the Swimming Drill Book

RUBEN GUZMAN

Human Kinetics

Library of Congress Cataloging-in-Publication Data

Guzman, Ruben J., 1957-
   The swimming drill book / Ruben Guzman.
      p. cm.
   Rev. ed. of: Swimming drills for every stroke. c1998.
   ISBN-13: 978-0-7360-6251-0 (soft cover)
   ISBN-10: 0-7360-6251-3 (soft cover)
   1. Swimming--Training. I. Guzman, Ruben J., 1957- Swimming drills for every stroke. II. Title.
   GV837.7.G89 2007
   797.2'1--dc22

                                        2006023900

ISBN-10: 0-7360-6251-3
ISBN-13: 978-0-7360-6251-0

Acquisitions Editor: Jana Hunter
Developmental Editors: Kase Johnstun and Kevin Matz
Assistant Editors: Laura Koritz and Cory Weber
Copyeditor: Joanna Hatzopoulos Portman
Proofreader: Erin Cler
Graphic Designer: Robert Reuther
Graphic Artist: Tara Welsch
Cover Designer: Andrew Tietz
Art Managers: Kelly Hendren and Kareema McLendon-Foster
Illustrators: Tim Offenstein and Roberto Sabas
Printer: Sheridan Books

Human Kinetics books are available at special discounts for bulk purchase. Special editions or book excerpts can also be created to specification. For details, contact the Special Sales Manager at Human Kinetics.

Printed in the United States of America   10   9   8   7   6   5   4   3   2

Human Kinetics
Web site: www.HumanKinetics.com

United States: Human Kinetics
P.O. Box 5076
Champaign, IL 61825-5076
800-747-4457
e-mail: humank@hkusa.com

Canada: Human Kinetics
475 Devonshire Road Unit 100
Windsor, ON N8Y 2L5
800-465-7301 (in Canada only)
e-mail: orders@hkcanada.com

Europe: Human Kinetics
107 Bradford Road
Stanningley
Leeds LS28 6AT, United Kingdom
+44 (0) 113 255 5665
e-mail: hk@hkeurope.com

Australia: Human Kinetics
57A Price Avenue
Lower Mitcham, South Australia 5062
08 8372 0999
e-mail: info@hkaustralia.com

New Zealand: Human Kinetics
Division of Sports Distributors NZ Ltd.
P.O. Box 300 226 Albany
North Shore City
Auckland
0064 9 448 1207
e-mail: info@humankinetics.co.nz

Contents

Drill Finder

Drill #	Drill	Stroke	Wet or dry	Action	Goal	Page #
1	Head and Body Position	All	Dry		Body position	2
2	Cannonball Float	All	Wet	Buoyancy	Body position	4
3	Dead Swimmer's Float	All	Wet	Buoyancy	Body position	6
4	Standing Streamline	All	Wet or dry		Body position	8
5	Streamline Float	All	Wet	Buoyancy	Body position	10
6	Sliding	All	Wet	Buoyancy	Body position	12
7	Sliding on Back	All	Wet	Buoyancy	Body position	14
8	Pencil Float	All	Wet	Buoyancy	Body position	16
9	Pencil Drop	All	Wet	Buoyancy	Body position	18
10	Over and Under Breathing	All	Wet	Breathing	Breathing	22
11	Flutter Kick Deck Drill	Backstroke, freestyle	Wet	Kicking	Mechanics	24
12	Vertical Flutter Kick	Backstroke, freestyle	Wet	Kicking	Mechanics, body position	26
13	Push and Float on Back	Backstroke	Wet	Buoyancy	Body position	28
14	Slow Flutter on Back	Backstroke	Wet	Kicking	Mechanics, body position	30
15	Streamline Back Flutter Kick	Backstroke	Wet	Kicking	Mechanics, body position	32
16	Slow Flutter on Front	Freestyle	Wet	Kicking	Mechanics, body position	34
17	Streamline Front Flutter Kick	Freestyle	Wet	Kicking	Mechanics, body position	36
18	Breaststroke Kick Deck Drill	Breaststroke	Dry	Kicking	Mechanics	38
19	Inverted Breaststroke Kick	Breaststroke	Wet	Kicking	Mechanics, body position, timing	40
20	Streamline Breaststroke Kick	Breaststroke	Wet	Kicking	Mechanics, body position, timing	42
21	Butterfly Kick Deck Drill	Butterfly	Dry	Kicking	Mechanics, timing	44

Drill #	Drill	Stroke	Wet or dry	Action	Goal	Page #
22	Underwater Dolphin Kick	Butterfly	Wet	Kicking	Mechanics, timing	46
23	Dolphin Drill	Butterfly	Wet	Kicking	Mechanics, body position, timing	48
24	Inverted Dolphin Kick	Butterfly	Wet	Kicking	Mechanics, timing	50
25	Streamline Inverted Dolphin Kick	Butterfly	Wet	Kicking	Mechanics, timing	52
26	Dolphin Tail Walk	Butterfly	Wet	Kicking	Mechanics, timing	54
27	Standing Whirlpools	All	Wet	Sculling	Feel for water	58
28	Sweep In, Sweep Out	All	Wet	Sculling	Feel for water	60
29	Deep-Water Scull	All	Wet	Sculling	Feel for water	62
30	Vertical Twists	All	Wet	Sculling	Feel for water	64
31	Somersaults	All	Wet	Sculling	Feel for water	66
32	Layout Drill	All	Wet	Sculling	Feel for water	68
33	Seated Drill	All	Wet	Sculling	Feel for water	70
34	Elementary Backstroke Pull	Backstroke	Wet	Sculling	Feel for water	72
35	Sea Otter	All	Wet	Sculling	Feel for water	74
36	Dog Paddle	All	Wet	Sculling	Feel for water	76
37	Front Scull	All	Wet	Sculling	Feel for water	78
38	Scull and Kick	All	Wet	Sculling	Feel for water	80
39	Lateral Scull	All	Wet	Sculling	Feel for water	82
40	Backstroke Recovery Deck Drill	Backstroke	Dry	Arms	Mechanics	86
41	Streamline Back Kick	Backstroke	Wet	Kicking, buoyancy	Body position	88
42	One-Arm Extended Back Kick	Backstroke	Wet	Kicking, buoyancy	Body position	90
43	The Sailboat Angle	Backstroke	Wet		Body position	92

Drill #	Drill	Stroke	Wet or dry	Action	Goal	Page #
44	Lateral Backstroke Kick	Backstroke	Wet	Kicking, buoyancy	Body position	94
45	Shoulder Roll Drill	Backstroke	Wet	Kicking, stroke	Body position, mechanics	96
46	Handshake Drill	Backstroke	Wet	Kicking, stroke, arms	Body position, mechanics, timing	98
47	Guided One-Arm Backstroke	Backstroke	Wet	Kicking, stroke, arms	Body position, mechanics, timing	100
48	Controlled One-Arm Backstroke	Backstroke	Wet	Kicking, stroke, arms	Body position, mechanics, timing	102
49	Double-Arm Backstroke	Backstroke	Wet	Kicking, stroke, arms	Mechanics	104
50	Controlled Two-Arm Backstroke	Backstroke	Wet	Kicking, stroke, arms	Body position, mechanics, timing	106
51	Continuous One-Arm Backstroke	Backstroke	Wet	Kicking, stroke, arms	Body position, mechanics, timing	108
52	Continuous Two-Arm Backstroke	Backstroke	Wet	Kicking, stroke, arms	Body position, mechanics, timing	110
53	Backstroke Final Adjustment	Backstroke	Wet	Arms	Mechanics	112
54	Streamline Freestyle Kick, No Breath	Freestyle	Wet	Kicking, buoyancy	Body position	116
55	One-Arm Extended Freestyle Kick	Freestyle	Wet	Kicking, buoyancy	Body position	118
56	Lateral Freestyle Kick	Freestyle	Wet	Kicking, buoyancy	Body position	120
57	Lateral Freestyle Breathe and Kick	Freestyle	Wet	Kicking, buoyancy, breathing	Body position, mechanics	122
58	Zip-Up	Freestyle	Wet	Kicking, arms	Body position, mechanics	124
59	Controlled One-Arm Freestyle	Freestyle	Wet	Kicking, stroke, arms	Body position, mechanics, timing	126
60	Controlled No-Breath Freestyle	Freestyle	Wet	Kicking, stroke, arms	Body position, mechanics, timing	128

Drill #	Drill	Stroke	Wet or dry	Action	Goal	Page #
78	Salmon Fly With Device	Butterfly	Wet	Kicking, stroke, arms	Mechanics, timing, breathing	168
79	Salmon Fly	Butterfly	Wet	Kicking, stroke, arms	Mechanics, timing	170
80	Standing Butterfly Arm Action	Butterfly	Dry	Arms	Mechanics	172
81	Butterfly Stroke Over Device	Butterfly	Wet	Kicking, stroke, arms	Mechanics, timing, breathing	174
82	Power Fly	Butterfly	Wet	Kicking, stroke, arms	Mechanics, timing	176
83	One-Arm Butterfly	Butterfly	Wet	Kicking, stroke, arms	Mechanics, timing, breathing	178
84	2 + 2 + 2	Butterfly	Wet	Kicking, stroke, arms	Mechanics, timing, breathing	180
85	Controlled Butterfly	Butterfly	Wet	Kicking, stroke, arms	Mechanics, timing, breathing	182
86	Streamline Jumps	All	Wet	Turns	Mechanics	186
87	Jump and Somersault	Backstroke, freestyle	Wet	Turns	Mechanics	188
88	Push-Off and Somersault	Backstroke, freestyle	Wet	Turns	Mechanics	190
89	One-Arm Extension and Flip	Backstroke, freestyle	Wet	Turns	Mechanics	192
90	Plus Kicking	Backstroke, freestyle	Wet	Turns	Mechanics	194
91	Plus 3 Strokes, Plus 3-Count Stretch	Backstroke, freestyle	Wet	Turns	Mechanics, timing	196
92	Backstroke Breakout	Backstroke	Wet	Turns	Mechanics, timing	198
93	Foot Touch	Backstroke, freestyle	Wet	Turns	Mechanics, timing	200
94	Freestyle-to-Backstroke Turn	Backstroke, freestyle	Wet	Turns	Mechanics, timing	202
95	Corkscrew Freestyle Breakout	Freestyle	Wet	Turns	Mechanics, timing	204
96	Freestyle Turn	Freestyle	Wet	Turns	Mechanics, timing	206
97	Backstroke Finish	Backstroke	Wet	Finish	Mechanics, timing	208

Drill #	Drill	Stroke	Wet or dry	Action	Goal	Page #
117	Push-Off Start From the Wall	Freestyle, breaststroke, butterfly	Wet	Starts	Mechanics	252
118	Dive From the Deck	Freestyle, breaststroke, butterfly	Wet	Starts	Mechanics	254
119	Dive From the Deck Plus Noodle	Freestyle, breaststroke, butterfly	Wet	Starts	Mechanics	256
120	Setup on the Blocks	Freestyle, breaststroke, butterfly	Wet	Starts	Mechanics	258
121	Dive From the Blocks	Freestyle, breaststroke, butterfly	Wet	Starts	Mechanics	260
122	Dive From the Blocks Plus Noodle	Freestyle, breaststroke, butterfly	Wet	Starts	Mechanics	262
123	Streamline Diving	Freestyle, breaststroke, butterfly	Wet	Starts	Mechanics	264
124	Butterfly Start	Butterfly	Wet	Starts	Mechanics, timing, body position	266
125	Breaststroke Start	Breaststroke	Wet	Starts	Mechanics, timing, body position	268
126	Freestyle Start	Freestyle	Wet	Starts	Mechanics, timing, body position	270
127	Backstroke Start Setup, Launch, and Entry	Backstroke	Wet	Starts	Mechanics, timing, body position	272
128	Backstroke Start	Backstroke	Wet	Starts	Mechanics, timing, body position	274

Foreword

Elite competitive swimmers today have a reputation for being among the hardest-training athletes in sports, but training hard is only part of the equation. To achieve the most success possible in your swimming career, you must work hard not only in training but also in improving your technique.

Refining and perfecting technique is a never-ending process. Age-group swimmers, senior swimmers, and elite swimmers alike must continually work on the proficiency of their strokes in order to make the greatest strides in their ability and performances. In these pages Ruben Guzman has supplied you with everything you need in order to do just that. *The Swimming Drill Book* is both an applicable training guide and a work of art. The descriptions, stroke components, and progressions are clearly written. The excellent illustrations bring the instruction to life and offer a visual example of how the drill should be executed.

Coaches and swimmers of all levels will enjoy the clear presentation, simple approach, and rewarding improvement that this book is sure to provide anyone who uses it. As a former Olympian, I am proud that our country continues to develop great coaches, innovators, and authors like Ruben, who are leaders in the quest to advance competitive swimming performance.

Pablo Morales
Five-time Olympic medalist
University of Nebraska head swim coach

Preface

In the past several years, since the writing of *Swimming Drills for Every Stroke*, there have been exciting new developments in understanding how the body can move more efficiently and fluidly through the water. Research also continues to show that the most significant factors in improved performance are technical—efficiency of the strokes, starts, and turns—rather than physical conditioning. *The Swimming Drill Book* incorporates those developments into a refined series of drills that have produced excellent results. In addition, the language of communicating these new concepts and skills to age-group and senior-level swimmers has been fine-tuned so that swimmers "get it" almost right away.

The book begins with a chapter on body position and buoyancy. Most of these concepts were derived from Dr. Bill Boomer, the U.S. Olympic team swimming guru. By simplifying the drills and developing a specific sequence of practicing the drills in daily workouts, swimmers have improved in efficiency from 25 to 40 percent.

A chapter on breathing and kicking and one on sculling will prepare swimmers for the chapters on each individual stroke. A new concept in the book is that of the body angle while swimming backstroke and freestyle. By using the sciences of physics and kinesiology, I have tested stroke efficiency to show that the optimal level of rotation is not 90 degrees—a popular notion—but approximately 45 degrees. The physics of the human body and its buoyancy are analogous to that of a sailboat, prompting the concept of the "sailboat angle" of rotation. From the kinesiological perspective, this is also consistent with maximum muscular power throughout the entire stroke cycle.

But improving in the pool isn't only about body position, breathing and kicking, and the strokes. Practicing starts, turns, and finishes also are important to the success of a swimmer, and the final three chapters provide an array of drills for every type of start, turn, and finish.

Coaches and swimmers at all levels can use this book to increase practice effectiveness, improve competitive times, and enhance fitness levels. Text to come!

Introduction

Swimming requires a combination of physical strength and technical finesse. Because the water is foreign to humans, the technical aspects of moving through it become much more critical at the competitive level. Most swimmers participating in the sport are relatively inexperienced in proper technique. For them, progress is most dramatic when their technique improves. But even for the most experienced swimmers, small technical improvements can make the difference between qualifying for nationals and not qualifying.

This book covers the fundamentals needed for competitive swimming. All of the essential drills are presented to assure that a swimmer is competent in the basics of competitive swimming. Mastering the basics provides the foundation for future development and refinement.

Swimmers need to have a planned approach to developing good technique that is simple to learn, and successfully proven and tested. Swimmers who use this book will benefit by learning effective ways to practice the skills of swimming. They will perform better and swim faster in competition. They are more likely to stay interested in swimming and will therefore enjoy the sport more.

Coaches need to have a well-planned, comprehensive curriculum. They also need a system that is flexible and can be adapted to a variety of situations. This book will benefit coaches by providing an organized approach to stroke instruction. By using this system, they can communicate the course outline more effectively in advance, thereby gaining support from swimmers and parents. Once a coach becomes skilled in using these drills, he or she can easily detect and correct stroke deficiencies, allowing the athletes to become faster and better swimmers.

Let's say you have sixteen weeks to prepare for a major competition. A good way to organize instruction is to divide drill training into three sections. Spend the first nine weeks teaching the drills presented in this book in sequential order. Cover one chapter a week. Next, repeat the drills in chapters 3-6 to polish and correct technique. This lasts four weeks. To wrap up, spend three weeks focusing on starts, turns, and finishes (chapters 7-9), along with brushing up any major stroke deficiencies.

Once you have your overall 16-week plan in place, organize each week like this:

- Day 1: Introduce the first two or three drills.
- Day 2: Review drills learned on Day 1, and then introduce two or three new drills.
- Day 3: Review all previously learned drills. Next teach the final set of drills.
- Days 4 and 5: Review all key drills in sequence.

Do your normal warm-up routine, but include at least one key drill learned the previous day. Once the entire system has been covered, a key drill from each stroke also becomes part of the warm-up. Each week, change the key drill. Key drills should be memorized by your swimmers and performed weekly.

To introduce and teach each drill, follow these steps:

- **Explain.** Provide a complete description of how the drill is performed.
- **Demonstrate.** Show how the drill is performed by using the diagrams, or demonstrate the drill yourself.
- **Correct.** Have swimmers perform the drill after your initial explanation and demonstration. Point out what is done correctly. Next, focus on one point at a time. Correct any errors until the drill is done properly.
- **Repeat.** Once the swimmers perform the drill correctly, repeat it until the drill becomes a habit. Make sure the swimmers do not develop improper techniques.

To coaches, your job is not an easy one and the rewards come all too slowly. I hope this material makes your job easier and more enjoyable.

To swimmers, my hope is that you enjoy performing these drills. There is so much to learn about swimming. Just learn it a little at a time. I hope this book helps you master all of the important skills and helps you swim easier and faster.

chapter 1

Body Position and Buoyancy

Water is not a natural environment for humans. To move through the water, we must learn to be relaxed and to have the water support our natural buoyancy—our ability to float. Being able to position the body for maximum buoyancy with minimum effort is fundamental to swimming faster.

These drills will

- enable you to feel how your body is positioned in the water,
- improve your ability to relax and have your body supported by the water,
- improve your ability to move through the water with less effort, and
- improve your efficiency in swimming all the strokes.

By learning how to relax and control body position, swimmers can improve their strokes almost instantly. While these drills may be simple to perform, they provide a transformational foundation for how swimmers experience their bodies in the water and for improvement in their performance. In fact, even experienced swimmers become much more efficient by practicing these drills. Whether you are a beginner or an international-level swimmer, these drills are fundamental to your success.

Purpose

To help you experience the different sections of the body and learn the importance of head position.

Procedure

1. Stand on deck with your back to a wall that is taller than you are.
2. Place your heels against the wall.
3. Push your hips back against the wall as well.
4. Tucking your chin in, place your shoulder blades back against the wall as well.
5. Gently move your head back to the point where the back of your head is touching the wall as well. You should have four contact points—heels, hips, shoulder blades, and head.
6. Take a small step away from the wall and try to maintain the same posture.
7. Step back against the wall to see whether you were successful.

Focus Points

- You will likely feel different than when in your normal standing posture. That's okay. Just feel how your body is lined up when the four contact points are touching the wall.
- Be sure to start with your heels and then move up to your hips, shoulder blades, and head.

Tips

- Practice standing or sitting with your ribs stretched upward. It will help you to maintain good posture in and out of the water.
- Perform the drill with a buddy who can correct you if you slouch.

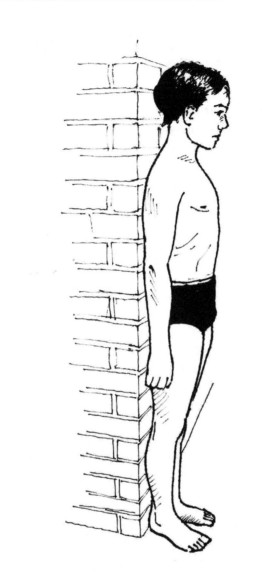

CANNONBALL FLOAT

Purpose

To give you a sense of how the body floats naturally and to help you feel the center of your buoyancy. This is the first key drill in the buoyancy series.

Procedure

1. Position yourself in the middle of a lane.
2. Inhale deeply, and hold your breath.
3. Bend at the hips and knees so that you can grab around your ankles.
4. Round your back, and tuck in your chin.
5. Allow your body to naturally float.
6. Hold this position as long as you can until you need to exhale.

Focus Points

- Be sure to inhale very deeply and hold your breath so you can float more easily.
- Keep the chin tucked in tightly.
- Feel which part of your back is floating highest at the surface.

Tips

- Try to keep your back at the surface as you draw your legs in underneath.
- Stay in the middle of the lane to avoid running into the lane rope.

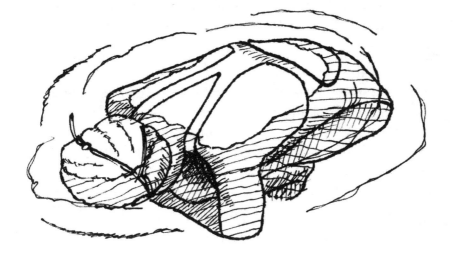

3   DEAD SWIMMER'S FLOAT

Purpose

To experience the natural buoyancy of the body while the arms and legs are completely relaxed. This is the second key drill in the buoyancy series.

Procedure

1. Position yourself in the middle of a lane.
2. As in the Cannonball Float, inhale deeply, and hold your breath.
3. Also, round your back and tuck your chin in.
4. Unlike in the Cannonball Float, completely relax your arms and legs. They should be completely limp, like wet spaghetti noodles.
5. Allow the body to naturally float.
6. Hold this position as long as you can until you need to exhale.

Focus Points

- Be sure to inhale deeply and hold your breath so you can float more easily.
- Keep your chin tucked in tight.
- Let your elbows and knees bend naturally; stay relaxed.
- Feel which part of your back is floating highest at the surface.

Tips

- Have your coach check your arms and legs to make sure they are relaxed.
- If you are practicing this drill at home or on your own, be sure to tell someone what you are doing so the person doesn't think you have drowned!

4   STANDING STREAMLINE

Purpose
To introduce the streamline arm position, the most important skill to master in competitive swimming. This drill will set up the next drills in the buoyancy series.

Procedure
1. Stand with your back against a wall.
2. Place your heels, hips, and shoulder blades against the wall as in the Head and Body Position drill.
3. Bring your chin down to allow your head to bend forward.
4. With your arms out in front of you, place one hand directly over the other with your fingers together. It does not matter which hand goes on top.
5. Wrap the thumb of the hand on top around the lower hand to lock your hands so that you cannot pull them apart.
6. Straighten your arms overhead so that your elbows are straight and your hands are against the wall.
7. Bring the head back to cradle against your arms. Now you are in a streamline.

Focus Points
- Be sure to hold your hands correctly: one hand over the other.
- Reach up and back so that your elbows are completely straight.
- Your head should be in front of your arms.
- You should feel four contact points against the wall: hands, shoulders, hips, and heels.

Tips
- Have your coach work with you to make sure you can do this drill standing away from the wall, and then in shallow water.
- Practice standing in front of a mirror to check your streamline position.

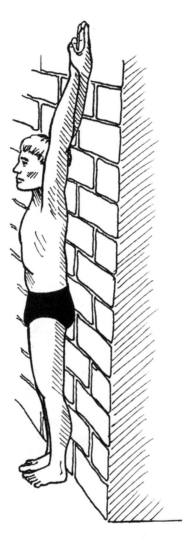

STREAMLINE FLOAT

Purpose

To learn how to stretch the body into the streamline position and reach maximum buoyancy—allowing the water to support the body. This exercise is by far the most difficult for many swimmers and may take extensive practice and body control to achieve. This is the third key drill in the buoyancy series.

Procedure

1. Position yourself in the middle of a lane.
2. Inhale deeply, and hold your breath.
3. Move into the Dead Swimmer's Float position (a).
4. Gradually extend the arms into the streamline position (b).
5. Gradually extend the legs and point the toes (c).
6. Give your body time to rise up to the surface.
7. Your goal is to have all four buoyancy points at the surface: hands, shoulders, hips, and heels (d).

Focus Points

- Be sure to keep your chin well tucked in.
- Do not force the float or try to kick your way up. Let the water support your body.
- If your legs start to sink, tighten your back and hips.

Tips

- Have your coach place a kickboard over your hips and heels so that you can feel when you have pushed them to the surface.
- Partner up with a buddy so that you can check each other.

6   SLIDING

Purpose

To develop control of buoyancy and body position while holding the streamline position. This is the fourth key drill in the buoyancy series.

Procedure

1. Position your body at the end of the lane, up against the wall and facing away from the wall. Your hands hold on to the gutter and your feet are up, ready to push off.
2. Inhale deeply, and hold your breath.
3. Push off from the wall at the surface in a streamline position.
4. Slide as far down the lane as possible.
5. Stop when your body has come to a complete stop to avoid running out of air.

Focus Points

- Be sure to push off at the surface, not below it.
- Make sure your head is tucked in underneath your arms.
- Keep your four buoyancy points at the surface: hands, shoulders, hips, and heels.
- Point your toes as you move through the water.
- Try to stay in the middle of the lane.

Tips

- In a group setting, combine swimmers from two lanes. Use one lane for sliding and the other lane for returning.
- On the way back, count the number of colored sections of the lane rope to measure your distance (count the number of sections past the flags). The farther you go, the better! The record for my team is all the way across a 25-yard pool!

Purpose

To develop control of buoyancy and body position while holding the streamline position on your back. This is the next key drill in the buoyancy series.

Procedure

1. Position your body at the end of the lane, facing the wall. Your hands hold on to the gutter and your feet are up, ready to push off (a).
2. Inhale deeply, and hold your breath.
3. Push off from the wall at the surface in a streamline on your back (b).
4. Slide as far down the lane as possible.
5. Stop when your body has come to a complete stop to avoid running out of air.

Focus Points

- Be sure to push off at the surface, not below it.
- Make sure your head is tucked in against your arms, with your face above the surface and your ears below the surface.
- Keep your main buoyancy point at the surface: the bottom of your rib cage.
- Point your toes as you move through the water.
- Try to stay in the middle of the lane.

Tips

- In a group setting, combine swimmers from two lanes. Use one lane for sliding and the other lane for returning.
- On the way back, count the number of colored sections of the lane rope to measure your distance. The farther you go, the better!

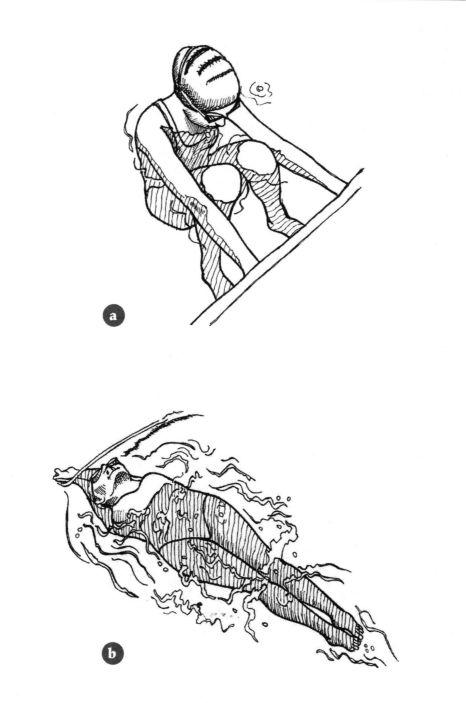

Purpose

To develop control of buoyancy and body position while holding a vertical position. This is an advanced buoyancy drill.

Procedure

1. While vertical, position your body in the middle of the lane.
2. Inhale deeply, and hold your breath.
3. Straighten your body, placing your hands at your sides (*a*).
4. Allow your body to naturally move down (*b*) and then up (*c*).
5. Tilt your head back as you come up so that you can quickly breathe.
6. Continue to breathe and float for at least 30 seconds.

Focus Points

- Be sure to take quick breaths.
- Point your toes.
- Try to keep your feet directly underneath you and stay in one place.

Tip

Position yourself over a particular spot in the pool and see if you can stay directly over it.

PENCIL DROP

Purpose
To develop a sense of when negative buoyancy occurs while holding a vertical position. This is an advanced buoyancy drill that follows the Pencil Float.

Procedure
1. While vertical, position your body in the middle of the lane.
2. Inhale deeply, and hold your breath.
3. Straighten your body, placing your hands at your sides *(a)*.
4. Exhale steadily until you begin to feel your body sink *(b)*.
5. Allow your body to sink to the bottom *(c)*.
6. Push off with your feet to return to the surface, and repeat the drill.

Focus Points
- Be sure to exhale smoothly.
- Some swimmers may need to let out very little air to begin sinking; others may need to let out a lot of air.
- Try to keep your feet directly underneath you and stay in one place.

Tips
- Position yourself over a particular spot in the pool, and try to stay directly over it.
- Partner up with a buddy. Notice how each of you is different in how quickly or slowly you sink.

chapter 2

Breathing and Kicking

Proper mechanics of breathing and kicking might be the simplest skills to perform in swimming. Yet these skills are often overlooked. Proper breathing and kicking are critical for swimmers to feel comfortable in the water, maintain good body position, and move through the water quickly and efficiently.

Fast and efficient swimmers

- kick through the water with the body in a streamline, or stretched position, and
- breathe comfortably and relaxed (holding the breath wastes energy).

The drills in this chapter will help you kick in a streamline position and learn proper breathing. Swimming with less drag and less friction saves energy and time. Correct kicking and breathing mechanics can often lead to dramatic results. This chapter is the next layer in the foundation for excellent swimming technique.

10   OVER AND UNDER BREATHING

Purpose
To ensure correct breathing. Breathing should flow in a relaxed manner; holding the breath wastes energy.

Procedure
1. Facing the wall or standing in shallow water, hold on to the gutter with both hands. Position your feet against the wall or on the bottom *(a)*.
2. Move your head up and down from just above the surface of the water to just below the surface *(b)*.
3. As soon as your mouth and nose go below the surface, breathe out and blow steady bubbles. Breathe in only when your mouth is above the surface.
4. Breathe slowly, and stay relaxed. Repeat the motion at least 20 times in a row.

Focus Point
Do not continue to breathe out when you lift your head up. If someone can hear you breathing out or if you spray water out of your mouth, then you need to concentrate on breathing out only underwater and breathing in only above water.

Tip
Place a lit candle (real or imaginary) in front of you above the surface. Don't blow out the candle!

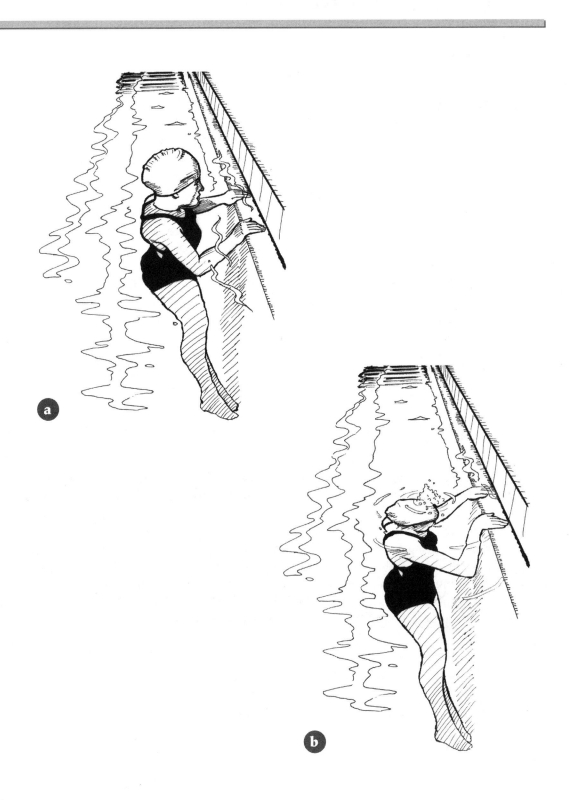

Purpose

To help you see and feel how to do the flutter kick.

Procedure

1. Sit on the edge of the deck. With your toes pointed and legs extended straight over the water, first touch just your toes to the surface of the water. Then, lower your legs so that your feet are about 12 inches under the water. Keep your legs close together.

2. Slowly raise one foot toward the surface, then lower it back 12 inches under the water while raising the other foot. Continue alternately raising and lowering your feet, making sure the feet are close together as they pass each other. Keep the toes pointed toward the opposite end of the pool.

3. Kick the water up toward the surface, but do not go above the surface. Gradually increase the speed of the kick.

4. As your speed increases, gradually bend your knees a little and relax the ankles.

Focus Points

- Keep your toes pointed toward the opposite end of the pool. Avoid pointing the toes up to the sky.
- "Boil" the water, but do not splash. Kick under the water, not in the air.

Tips

- Ask someone to stand in the water and hold his or her hand just under the water with his or her palm facing the pool floor. Kick the palm flat with the top of your foot. If your toes hit first, they need to be pointed more.
- Practice leg raises. Holding on to a bar or the back of a chair, stand straight with one foot flat on the ground. Point the toes of the other foot, and touch the big toe to the ground. Keeping your leg straight, lift it about 12 inches off the ground. Hold the position for 2 seconds. Slowly lower your leg and touch the big toe to the ground. Repeat 10 to 20 times. Switch legs.

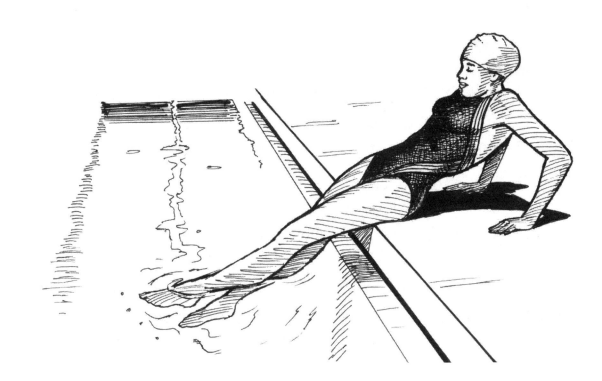

Purpose

To help swimmers develop the full power of the flutter kick. Vertical kicking is perhaps the quickest way to develop a powerful, efficient kick.

Procedure

1. Position yourself vertically in deep enough water that your toes cannot touch the bottom of the pool.
2. Face the lane rope, and hold on to it with your arms extended.
3. Begin to slowly flutter kick, keeping your body at a vertical position with good posture (a). Your feet should only separate about 12 inches.
4. Gradually kick a little harder so that your shoulders come above the surface (b, c).

Focus Points

- Keep your knees fairly straight.
- Maintain excellent posture. Many swimmers tend to push the hips back, so focus on keeping them straight and staying completely erect.
- Keep your feet moving quickly back and forth with smaller separation. Avoid bending your hips and knees and doing a bicycle kick.

Tips

- When you are able, try kicking in the vertical position with sculling (see chapter 3).
- For an added challenge, bring your hands above the surface.
- For an extreme challenge, add a weight belt!

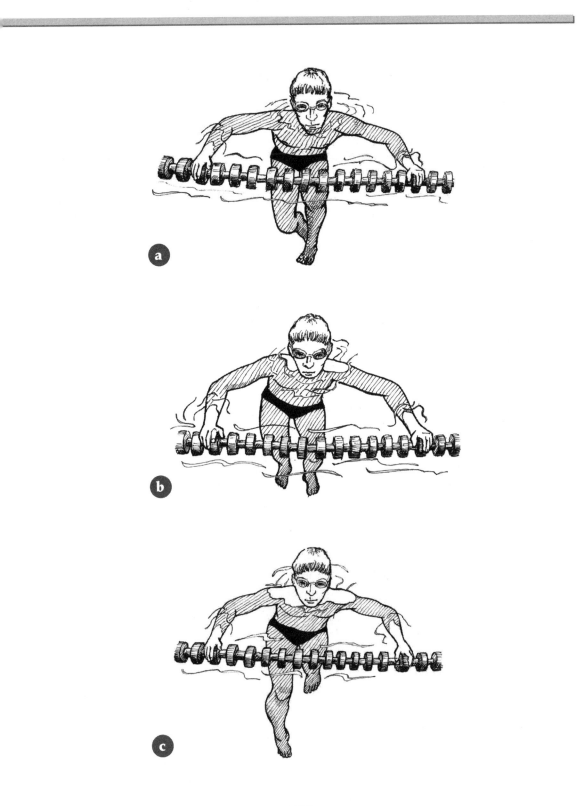

Purpose

To establish the feel for the proper body position for the backstroke.

Procedure

1. Hold on to the gutter or wall, and place your feet on the wall at around hip depth (a).
2. Let go of the wall, and slowly push off using your legs. Straighten your body, and float along the surface for about 5 seconds.
3. Keep your arms at your sides. Arch your back a little so that your abdomen stays up along the surface. Feel how the bottom of your rib cage is up. It's okay if your legs sink a little (b).
4. Breathe comfortably, keeping your upper body on the surface.

Focus Points

- Feel the bottom of your rib cage staying up at the surface.
- Be sure to keep your head back far enough that your ears are just under the water.
- Point your toes as you float.

Tip

Ask someone to place a half-board or noodle on your abdomen as you begin to float. See how long you can keep it there.

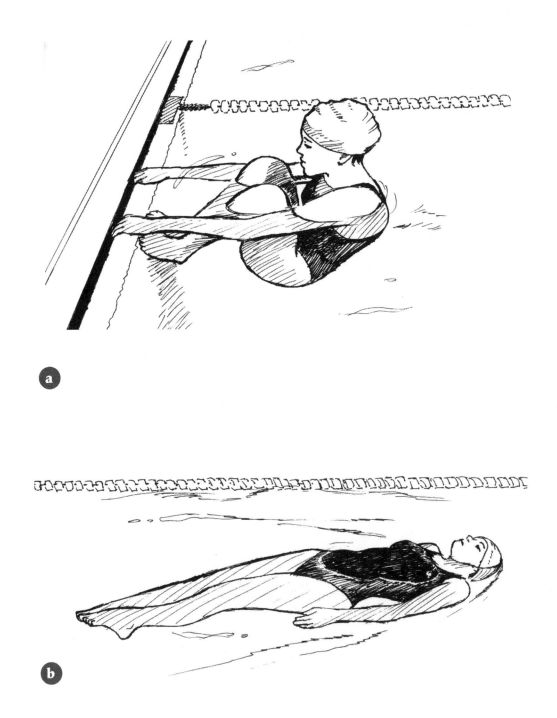

Purpose

To practice correct body position for the backstroke while adding a kicking action.

Procedure

1. Begin with the floating position as in drill 13 (Push and Float on Back), and gradually add a slow flutter kick. Kick just fast enough to keep the bottom of your rib cage at the surface *(a, b)*.
2. Kick a lap.
3. Stop before you get to the wall.

Focus Points

- Kick as slowly as possible while maintaining correct body position.
- Stay relaxed! Keep your head back, and enjoy yourself.

Tip

Ask someone to place a half-board or noodle on your abdomen as you begin to kick. See how long you can keep it there.

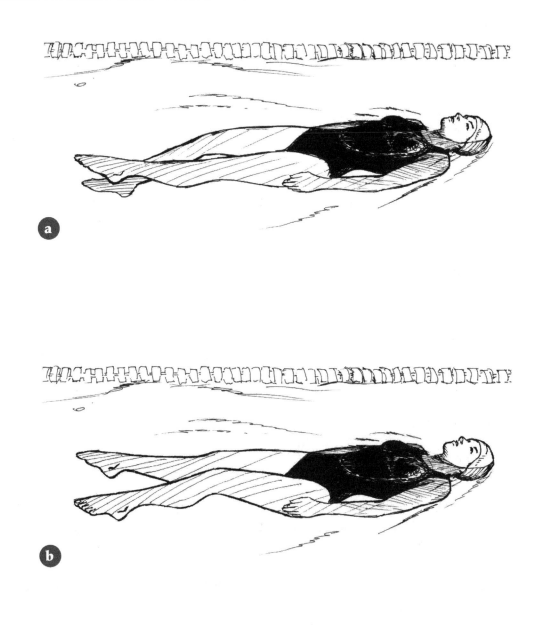

Purpose

To introduce the streamline arm position with kicking. Maintaining a good streamline will reduce friction and help you slice through the water with very little energy.

Procedure

1. Place one hand over the other with your fingers together. It does not matter which hand goes on top.
2. Wrap the thumb of the hand on top around the lower hand to lock your hands so that you cannot pull them apart (a).
3. Straighten your arms overhead so that you cradle or brace your head between your arms. Your arms should be at least slightly behind your ears with the elbows completely locked (b).
4. Push off the wall to a floating position as in drill 13 (Push and Float on Back), but hold a streamline position.
5. Gradually add a slow kick while keeping your abdomen up with the bottom of the rib cage as your focus point. Think in the following pattern: float, streamline, kick (c).

Focus Points

- Concentrate on each aspect in this order: float, streamline, kick.
- Relax; don't force it.
- Keep your toes pointed and your ankles relaxed.
- Kick slowly.
- Keep your head back.
- Keep your hands just under the water.

Tips

- Using a kickboard or noodle as described in drill 13 (Push and Float on Back) works well here.
- Stand in front of a mirror to check your streamline position.
- There are three rules for an excellent streamline. Commit these rules to memory:
  1. Place one hand over the other.
  2. Lock the thumb.
  3. Brace the head.

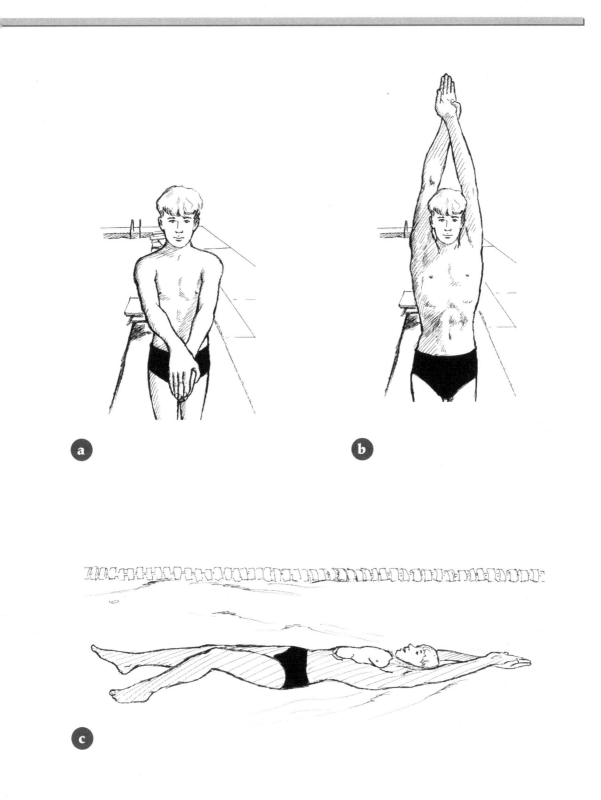

Purpose

To practice correct body position for the freestyle while adding a kicking action.

Procedure

1. Starting at the wall, take a deep breath.
2. Push off from the wall with your eyes facing down, just the back of your head touching the surface. You should also feel your shoulders, hips, and heels at the surface.
3. Gradually add a slow flutter kick. Kick just fast enough to keep your hips touching the surface.
4. Kick as far as you can and slowly exhale until you need to breathe; then stop, breathe, and repeat.

Focus Points

- Kick as slowly as possible while maintaining correct body position.
- Feel your hips touching the surface at all times.
- Kick the water, not the air. If you can hear your kick, the feet are coming up too high.
- Stay relaxed!

Tips

- Have your coach or a partner place a half-board or noodle just above the hips to see if you can carry it forward.
- Imagine you are snorkeling and looking at all the fish at the bottom of the ocean!
- Do this with the FINIS Snorkle.

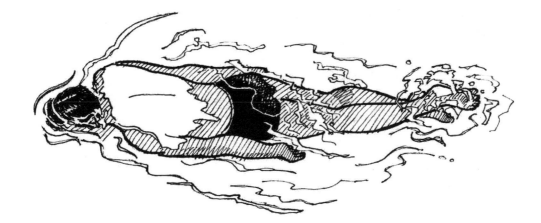

Purpose

To develop good kicking mechanics while kicking freestyle on your front side. This position is frequently used in training sets.

Procedure

1. Starting at the wall, take a deep breath.
2. Push off the wall, and place your hands in a prone streamline position. Keep your hands, shoulders, hips, and heels at the surface.
3. Slide for 2 seconds. Then, begin kicking with a quick, steady flutter kick. Keep your toes in the water at all times. The heels of your feet should just barely break the surface of the water. Your hips should be right at the surface (a).
4. Keep your head tucked in under your arms. Slowly exhale to let your air out and go as far as you can, then stop. Breathe, and repeat (b).

Focus Points

- Keep your arms in the streamline position.
- Kick the water, not the air. In other words, avoid lifting your feet above the surface of the water. While the splashing may look impressive, it does nothing but waste energy.
- Keep your hips up.

Tips

- Try to position your head so that it is just barely breaking the surface or is slightly below the surface. It will help get you ready for the freestyle drills.
- Do this with the FINIS Snorkle.

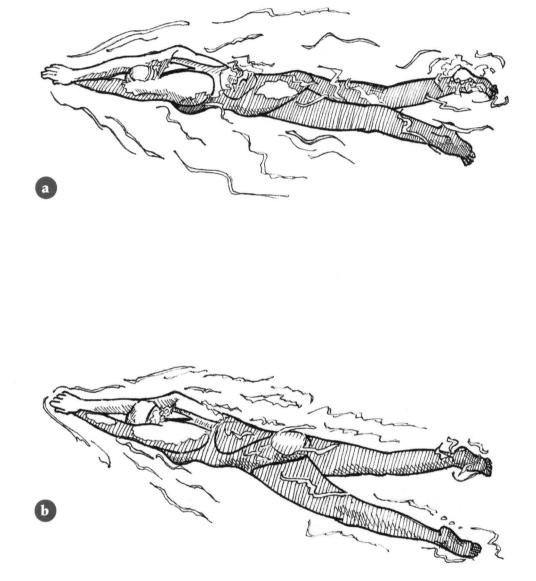

Purpose
To help swimmers see and feel how a proper breaststroke kick is done.

Procedure
1. Sit on the edge of the deck with your legs extended over the water. Keep your heels just below the surface at all times during this exercise. Begin with your legs together and toes pointed, the inner sides of your feet touching (a).
2. Bring the legs in toward your body (flex at the knees and draw your thighs upward) so that the knees are about shoulder-width apart, the heels are close together, and the toes point to the sides of the pool (b).
3. Rotate your feet out to catch the water with the inner sides of the feet, keeping the knees about shoulder-width apart (c).
4. Begin to squeeze the water between your legs while keeping your feet flexed (d).
5. Bring your legs completely together, and finish with your toes pointed. You should see and feel the powerful squeeze of the water.

Focus Points
- Develop the following pattern: in, out, squeeze, together.
- Be sure to finish each kick with the knees straight and the toes pointed.
- Catch as much water as possible on the sides of your feet when you squeeze your legs together.

Tips
- You can practice this kick almost anywhere. Try it while sitting down on the floor watching television. Or you can sit on your bed and practice it before you go to sleep.
- For an advanced version, begin in a leg lift position and do not let the feet touch. This variation is great for the abdominals!

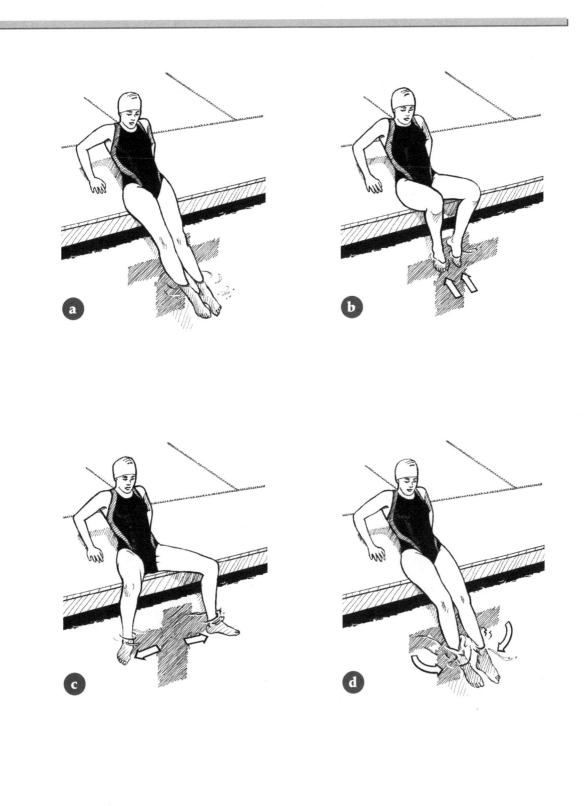

Purpose
To develop a balanced breaststroke kick with good body control. This drill helps to prevent exaggerated hip action and improper leg mechanics. Anyone with a weak breaststroke kick should emphasize this drill.

Procedure
1. Start by pushing off the wall to float on your back into a streamline position along the surface (a). Be sure to float and keep your chest up!
2. After counting to three (one thousand one, one thousand two, one thousand three), begin and complete a breaststroke kick (b).
3. Count to three between each repetition.

Focus Points
- Keep your upper-body position stable. Your head and chest should not go under the water. If they do, it usually means you are not keeping your feet up high enough.
- Keep a tight streamline. Your hands should stay just below the surface.
- Finish each kick with the body in a floating position with the chest up and the toes pointed and near the surface.
- Do not allow your knees to rise more than 1 inch above the surface.

Tip
Move across the pool with as few kicks as possible. Make it a contest with a friend!

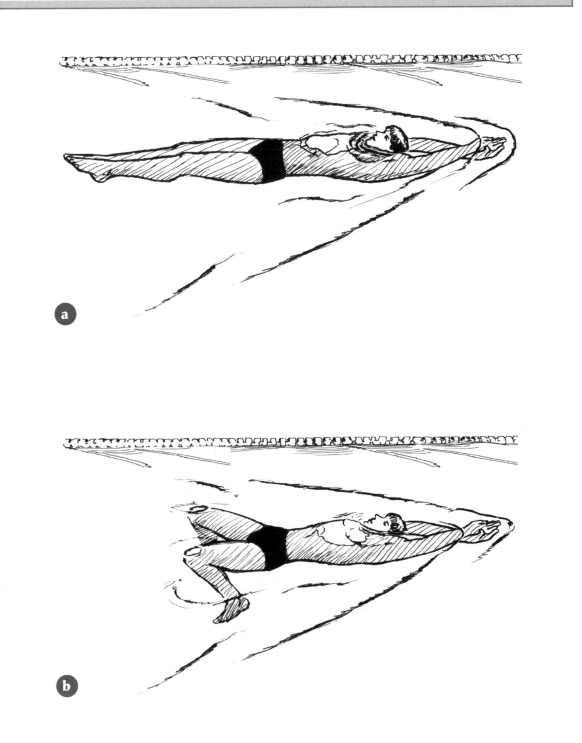

Purpose

To progress in the development of the breaststroke kick.

Procedure

1. Starting at the wall, take a deep breath.
2. Push off the wall, and place your hands in a prone streamline position. Keep your hands, shoulders, hips, and heels at the surface.
3. Slide for 2 seconds. Then begin kicking the breaststroke kick with a three-count hold in between (*a, b*). When you finish the kick, you should feel your hips up at the surface. The heels of your feet should just barely break the surface of the water (*c*).
4. Keep your head tucked in under your arms. Slowly exhale to let your air out and go as far as you can, then stop. Breathe, and repeat.

Focus Points

- Keep your arms in a tight streamline with your head tucked in underneath.
- Finish each kick with a tight squeeze and your toes pointed.
- Each time you keep your feet together for a count of three is called a slide. You'll need to remember this for later drills.
- Keep your knees from drifting wider than shoulder-width apart.

Tips

- Have someone watch to make sure you are squeezing the kick and keeping your hips up at the end of each kick.
- Move across the pool with as few kicks as possible.

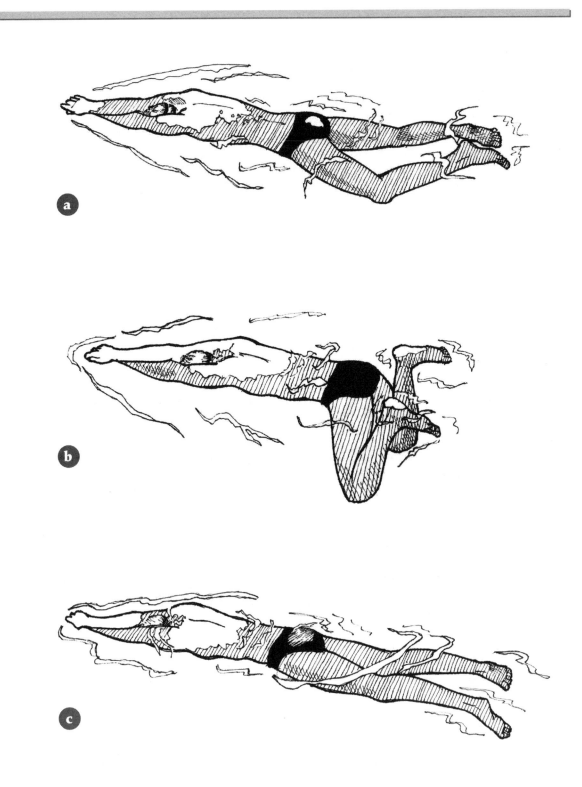

Purpose

To feel the body action of the butterfly stroke.

Procedure

1. Stand on the deck with your hands on your hips. Be sure to keep good back posture at all times during this exercise—avoid rounding the back and shoulders. Always look forward.

2. Begin by pushing your hips back and your chest forward while keeping your back and legs straight. (The correct position will feel a little like starting to lean over to get a drink of water from a drinking fountain.) Push your hips as far back as you can while still maintaining your balance (a).

3. Return your hips to a straight position. Push your hips forward, bending your knees slightly and keeping your back slightly arched (b). Once again return to the straight position.

4. Once you are comfortable with the motions, start to blend them in a smooth, continuous action. Try to feel your hips moving through a full range of motion.

Focus Points

- Be sure to keep your neck flexible so that you always look forward. Your chin should be tucked in when your hips are forward and should stick out when your hips are back.
- Keep a slight arch in your low back at all times.
- At first, push the hips as far forward and back as possible. Then, speed it up and move your hips just a few inches forward and a few inches back.

Tips

- Practice in front of a mirror at home so that you can see that you are always looking forward.
- Do this drill in shallow water (about waist high), and really feel how the water moves.

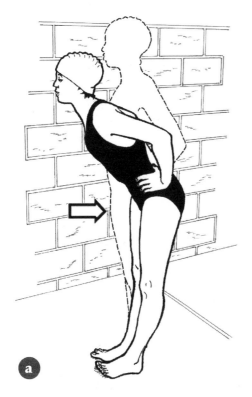

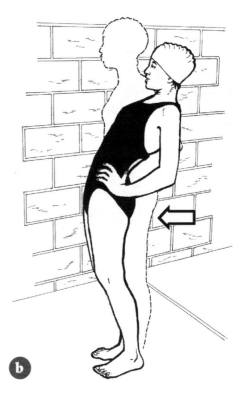

Purpose

To feel the complete body action of the butterfly.

Procedure

1. Put on fins. Imagine yourself as a mermaid (or merman) swimming along easily under the sea.
2. Take a deep breath. Then, push off the wall on your front side under the surface, keeping your hands down by your sides and looking down at the bottom of the pool. Do not use your arms at all on this drill.
3. Use your head to start the body action (a). Push downward with the forehead to start the whiplike action of the kick. Keep the head angle changing, but primarily look down (b, c).

Focus Points

- Do the surface dive very slowly. Really feel your body slide into the deeper water.
- Be sure to keep your head moving at all times.
- Look down at the black line on the bottom of the pool. If you are looking forward, your hips will not be able to create enough power for a strong kick.

Tips

- Have someone watch you under the water to see that you are not looking forward.
- Use a FINIS Monofin to help you get the body action of the kick.

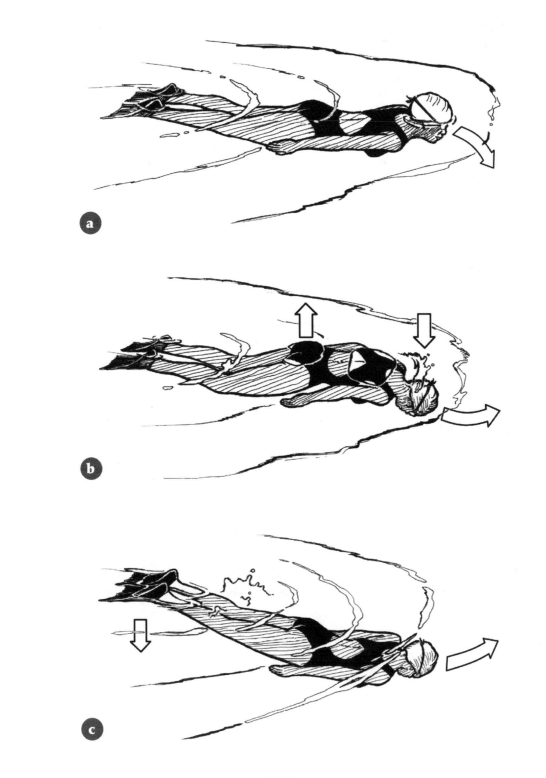

Purpose

To feel the body action of the butterfly stroke while at the surface.

Procedure

1. Put on fins. Imagine yourself as a dolphin swimming at the surface on the ocean. This drill will have the same body action as the previous drill, except at the surface.

2. Take a deep breath. Push off of the wall on your front side along the surface, keeping your hands down by your sides and looking down at the bottom of the pool (a). Just the back of your head will break the surface. Do not use your arms on this drill.

3. Use your head to start the body action. Push downward with the forehead to start the whiplike action of the kick (b). Keep the head angle changing, but primarily look down. As you push your forehead down, allow the hips to come up (c). Then, allow your feet to slide above the surface, and begin to kick down (d). Your head will begin to come back up to break the surface as you kick down.

4. Break the surface with your head, and repeat.

5. Your body will "stitch" the surface of the water. Your head, then back, then hips, and then feet will all break the surface in progression with each kick. Keep the motion fluid.

6. Go as far as you can with one breath, breathe, and then repeat.

Focus Points

- Be sure to keep your head moving at all times.
- Look down at the black line on the bottom of the pool. If you are looking forward, your hips will not be able to create enough power for a strong kick.
- Remember to move with your forehead first.
- Develop a steady rhythm.

Tip

Stay relaxed and see if you can make it all the way across the pool without having to stop and breathe.

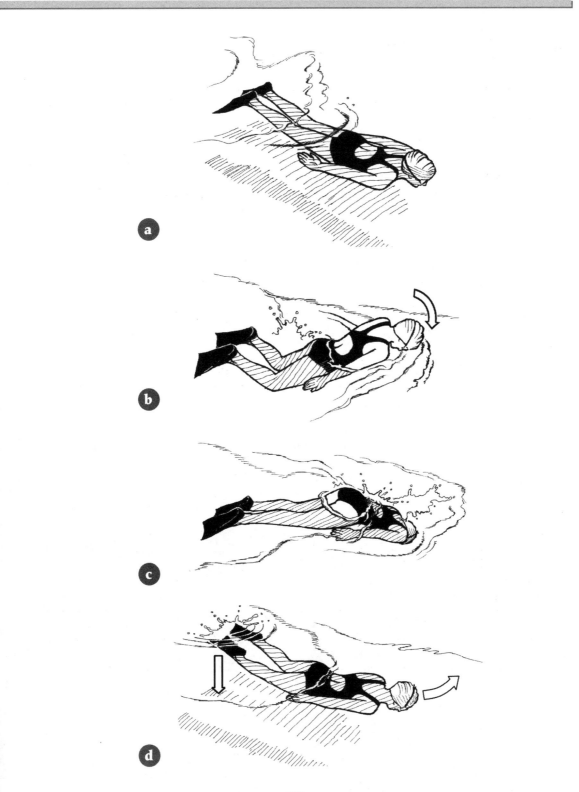

Purpose
To practice the body action of the butterfly stroke.

Procedure
1. Put on fins. Push off the wall, and float on your back with your arms down at your sides.
2. Begin the dolphin kick by pushing your abdominals up (*a*). Then, progressively push your knees, and then your feet, up to the surface, creating a whiplike action beginning with the abdominals (*b*). Your hands and head may go up and down a little; that's okay. Be sure to put one hand above your head to protect it as you approach the wall.

Focus Points
- Be sure to push the abdominals up above the surface on each kick.
- Kick from the hips, not the knees, bending your knees just a little.

Tips
- Start off underwater, then gradually come to the surface. See if the kick feels the same.
- Do slow, big, powerful kicks at first. Build speed later.

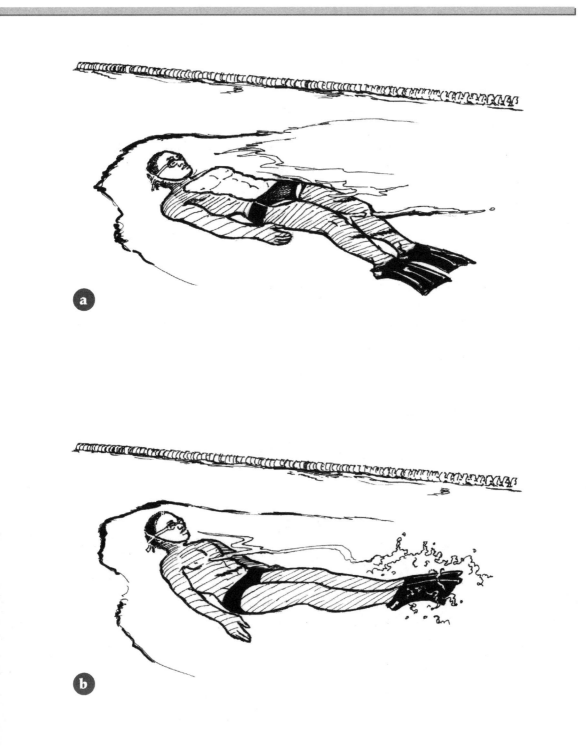

Purpose

To practice the body action of the butterfly stroke.

Procedure

1. Put on fins. Push off the wall, and float on your back with your arms above your head in a streamline position (a).
2. Begin the dolphin kick by pushing your abdominals, then knees, and finally your feet up to the surface (b).

Focus Points

- Be sure to push your abdominals up above the surface on each kick.
- Kick from the hips, not the knees, bending your knees just a little.

Tips

- Start off underwater, then gradually come to the surface. See if the kick feels the same.
- Do slow, big, powerful kicks at first. Gradually build speed. As you get faster, the kicks will be shallower and quicker.

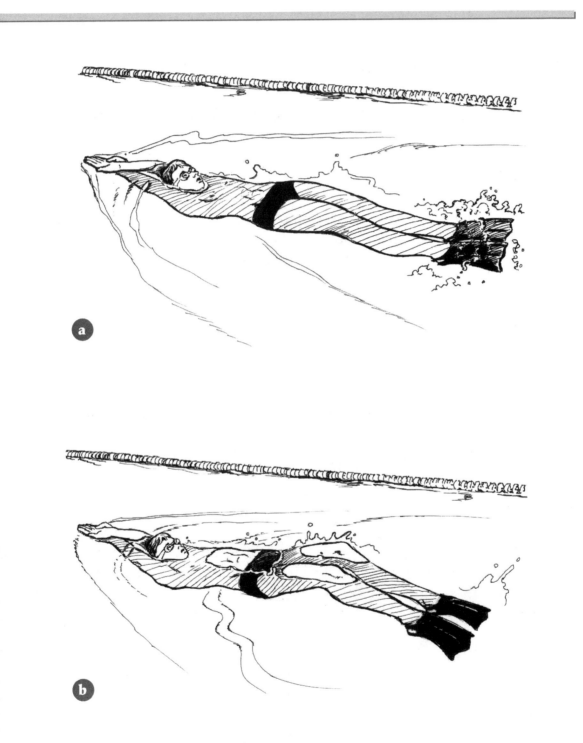

Purpose

To feel the body action, speed, and power of the butterfly kick.

Procedure

1. First, imagine watching the dolphins like you would see at a marine park. Picture the dolphins as they kick up above the surface and seem to walk backward on the surface with their tails. Their bodies move back and forth quickly and powerfully as they gradually move backward. You will now attempt to imitate this movement.

2. Put on fins. Push off the wall on your back, with feet deep, arms down at your sides, and head above the surface. Use quick, strong dolphin kicks to keep your head and shoulders above the water as you gradually kick backward (a). This one is a challenge! You will really feel your abdominals!

Focus Points

- Feel the hips working back and forth as quickly and powerfully as possible.
- Kick from the hips, not the knees, bending the knees just a little.

Tips

- For an advanced version, keep your hands just above the surface at your sides (b).
- To build great power, try the drill while wearing a weight belt.

 *chapter 3*

Sculling

For effective arm action in all the strokes, swimmers need to learn how to generate propulsion through the shape of their hands and forearms as they move through the water. Sculling drills may be the best way of learning the propeller-like propulsion methods that swimming scientists have long considered the most effective.

These drills are a practical way to

- practice pulling action, lifting action, and the finish of all strokes;
- learn about the pitch, lift, and angles of attack—creating whirlpools gives you direct feedback;
- improve your feel for the water; and
- strengthen your hands, forearms, and wrists.

By modifying the body's position and the direction of the sculling, swimmers can feel how to apply pressure in the water and position their fingers, hands, wrists, and forearms for the most effective movement. These drills offer a basic beginning to the art of sculling.

Purpose

To develop the foundation for propulsive arm movement in all the strokes. This drill presents the basic sculling action. The drills that follow use this basic action in some fun and challenging positions.

Procedure

1. Stand in water about shoulder depth. Start with one arm extended with the hand about 12 inches deep (a).
2. With your palm facing downward and your wrist strong, begin to trace a figure eight on its side. Sweep up and out, then sweep down and in (b, c). This is the basic sculling action.
3. Your hand should move across only about 12 to 18 inches. These movements are short but strong.
4. Keep the pressure on the palm of the hand. Use enough pressure to create a whirlpool at the surface.
5. Switch hands, and repeat.

Focus Points

- Quickly change the angle of your hand as you move it back and forth.
- Keep your wrists strong.
- Rotate from the elbow.
- Feel the pressure on the hand and forearm.

Tip

Practice sculling with different hand shapes: a fist, two fingers, fingers together, fingers spread, and fingers together with the thumb out.

Purpose

To develop coordination in sculling with both hands and to improve feel for the water.

Procedure

1. Stand in water about shoulder depth. Start with both arms extended in front of you about 12 inches deep.
2. Next, using the same action as the previous drill, scull with the hands moving in opposite directions at the same time. Sweep out with both hands to a little wider than shoulder-width (*a*), then sweep in with both hands (*b*).
3. Start slowly, and gradually move your hands more quickly to create two whirlpools.

Focus Points

- Quickly change the angle of the hands as you move them through the water.
- Keep your wrists strong.
- Rotate from the elbow.
- Feel the pressure on the hands and forearms.

Tips

- Practice sculling with different hand shapes: a fist, two fingers, fingers together, fingers spread, and fingers together with the thumb out.
- Move to deep water and see if you can create the whirlpools at the surface while you flutter kick and stay in a vertical position.

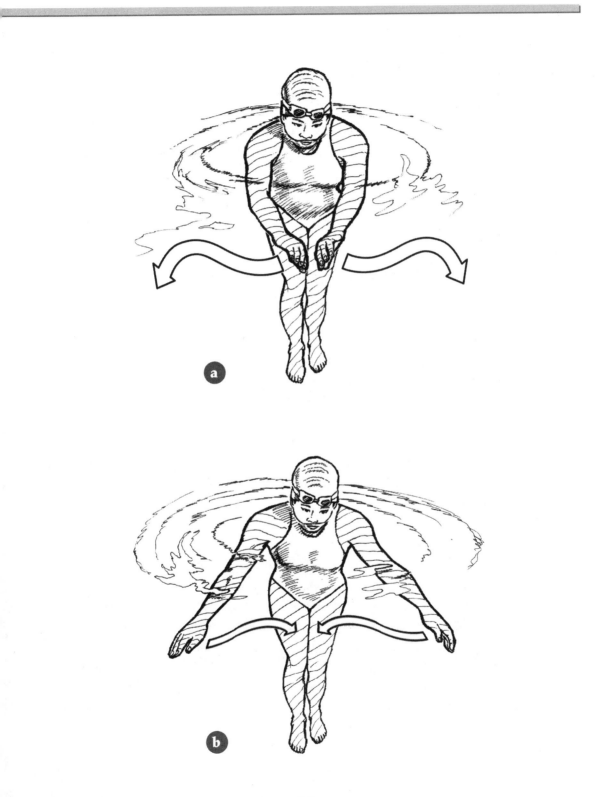

a

b

Purpose
To practice the sculling motion.

Procedure
1. Move to deep water, where your feet cannot touch the bottom.
2. Practice the basic two-hand sculling action, and keep your feet together *(a, b)*. Be sure to keep your head up and your body straight. Create whirlpools at the surface.
3. Start by sculling just 20 seconds at a time, then try to gradually increase the amount of time to several minutes. It's a tough workout!

Focus Points
- Move your hands quickly.
- Keep your body straight.
- Keep your feet together.
- Keep your head up.

Tips
- For variety, change your body position very slowly while keeping the hand action very fast.
- Try any arm position, but don't kick.

Purpose

To practice body control while sculling.

Procedure

1. Start in deep water, where your feet do not touch the bottom. Begin with the basic sculling action with both arms extended out at your sides.
2. While sculling with short, quick hand movements and changing the angle of your hands, begin to rotate slowly in one direction for a couple of turns, and then reverse the direction (*a*).
3. Next, rotate with one hand behind your back, using short, quick hand movements (*b*). Alternate the directions of rotation.

Focus Points

- Rotate slowly with short, quick hand movements.
- Keep your body straight.
- Keep your feet together.
- Keep your head up.

Tips

- If you have trouble staying up, try using a pull buoy between your legs.
- For an advanced variation, try doing this drill upside-down, with the feet above the surface.

Purpose

To feel the hands and forearms acting as oars.

Procedure

1. Start in deep water where your feet do not touch the bottom, preferably at least 6 feet deep so you don't hit your head on the bottom. Sink just under the water, and tuck into a tight ball, keeping your chin tucked into your chest.
2. Extend your arms out to your sides. Keep the arms almost completely straight *(a)*.
3. Begin to somersault forward, moving your arms quickly (sculling) in a circular motion *(b)*.
4. If you are able, do two or three somersaults in a row.
5. Try doing reverse somersaults as well.

Focus Points

- Keep your arms extended.
- Keep your chin tucked in.
- Keep the sculling action of the hands short and quick.
- Rotate slowly.

Tip

Breathe out slowly so that water does not go up your nose.

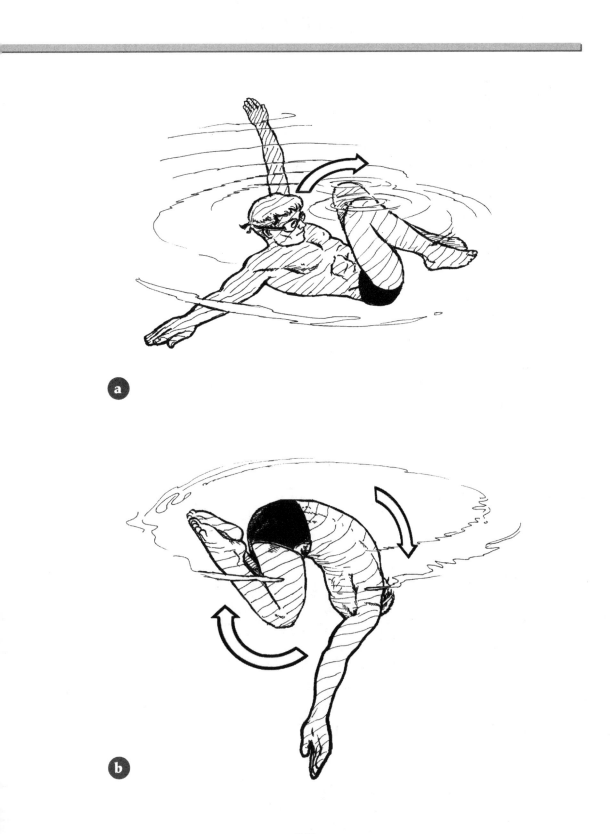

Purpose

To practice the wrist action needed for all strokes.

Procedure

1. Float on your back with your toes pointed, feet together, and abdominals up. You will be traveling headfirst.
2. Keep your arms straight with your hands down at your sides, and scull the water under the hips *(a, b)*.
3. Use a quick wrist action.

Focus Points

- Keep your arms straight and focus on working the wrists.
- Keep your abdominals up.
- Keep your feet pointed and at the surface.
- Use quick hand action.

Tip

For an advanced version, try going feet first. Use just the wrists, and try not to bend the elbows.

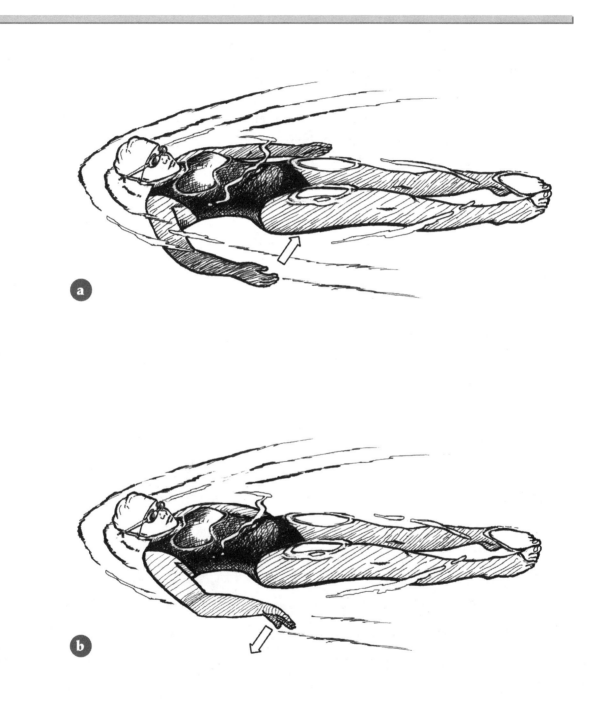

Purpose

To practice the wrist action needed for all strokes.

Procedure

1. Begin by floating on your back, then tuck into a seated position. Keep your knees and toes at the surface. Your head should be up as well.
2. Scull the water inward so that it travels under your knees (a). You will travel backward.
3. Use a quick wrist action (b).

Focus Points

- Keep your arms extended, and focus on working the wrists.
- Keep your knees up at the surface.
- Stay in a seated position.

Tip

For an advanced version, travel feet first. Use just the wrists, and try not to bend the elbows. In the forward direction, scoop backward under your hips.

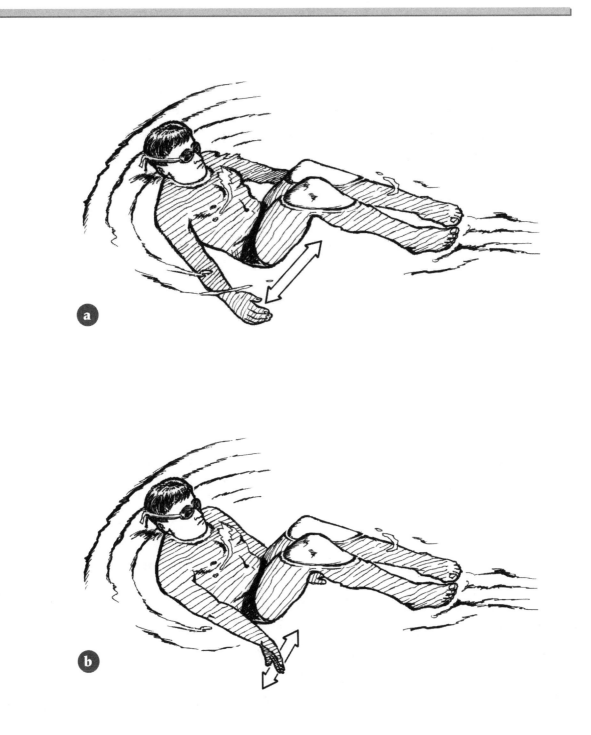

Purpose

To practice the backstroke pulling action.

Procedure

1. Begin by floating flat on your back, traveling headfirst.
2. Keeping your hands under the water at all times, place your arms over your head, palms facing out.
3. Using both arms at the same time, pull downward past the shoulders, keeping the arms fairly straight (*a*).
4. Begin to bend your elbows and turn your palms down toward your knees (*b*).
5. Keeping your hands close to the surface, continue to pull the water down toward your knees, and finish the pull with your thumbs against your thighs (*c*).
6. Then return your hands to the starting position by drawing them up alongside your body and stretching your arms overhead. Remember to keep your arms underwater.

Focus Points

- Pull evenly and slowly. Feel the pressure on the palms and forearms.
- Stay flat on your back with your abdominals up.

Tip

Use a pull buoy between your legs if it helps.

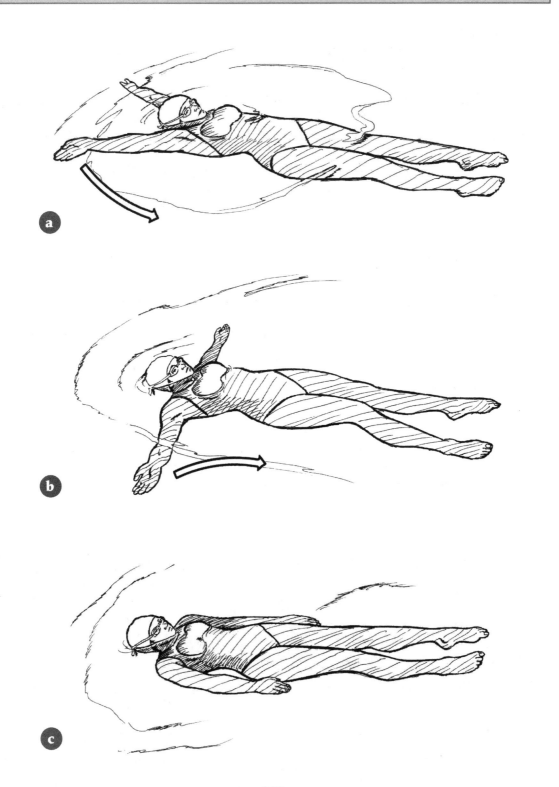

Purpose

To practice the feel of the finish of the strokes.

Procedure

1. Begin floating on your front side. You will travel headfirst. Keep your head up.
2. Place your arms down at your sides, keeping your elbows close to your ribs.
3. Bend your elbows so your hands are under your waist. Using your hands and forearms, scull the water backward, beginning at the waist (a).
4. Create a small circular motion with the sculling. Move your hands very quickly (b).

Focus Points

- Keep your elbows in.
- Keep your head up as high as possible so that your eyes remain above the surface.
- Keep your hands under your waist.

Tips

- Using a pull buoy between your legs may help.
- Try sculling both forward and backward.

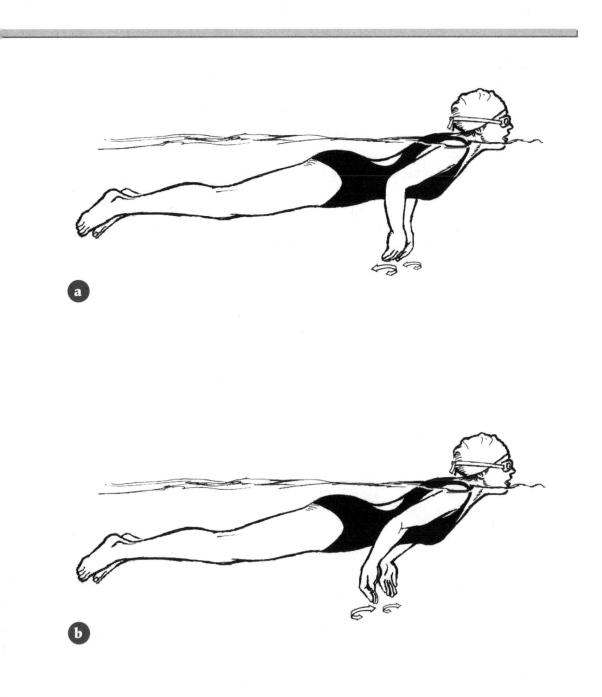

Purpose

To practice the feeling of the lift needed from the middle of the strokes.

Procedure

1. Begin floating on your front side, traveling headfirst. Keep your head up.
2. Your hands should be deep in the water, and your elbows should stay under your shoulders.
3. Bend your elbows, and put your hands under your chin.
4. Alternating arms, scull down and back until your arms are straight and your hands are below your chest. Then, bend your elbow, and bring your hand up toward your body, then forward under your chin (*a*). Keep your hands above your waist, and move them very quickly (*b*).

Focus Points

- Keep your elbows in a steady position under the shoulders.
- Keep your head up so that your eyes remain above the surface.
- Keep your hands above your waist.

Tip

Using a pull buoy between your legs may help.

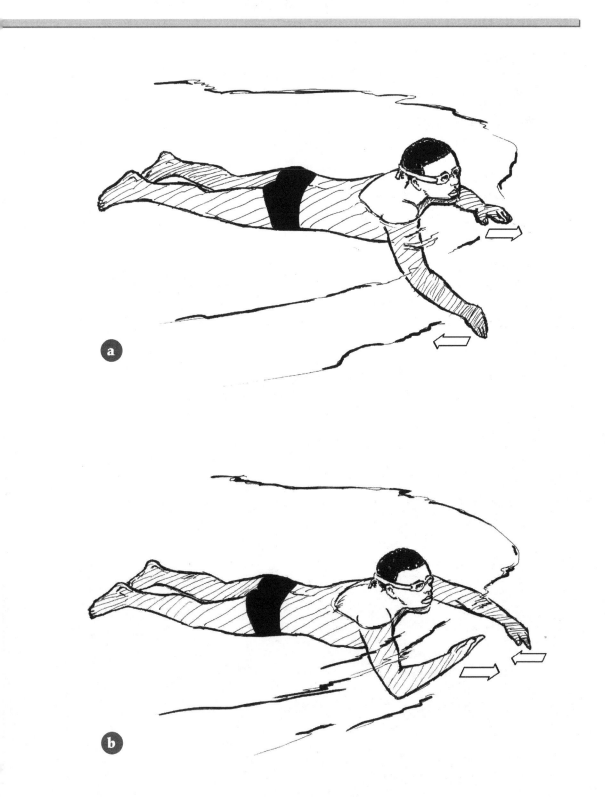

Purpose

To practice feeling the catch of the water at the beginning of the pulling action for the strokes.

Procedure

1. Begin floating on your front side, traveling headfirst. Keep your head up.
2. Extend your arms in front of you. Sweep them out (*a*), then press them in using a wide motion (*b*).
3. Move your arms very quickly.
4. Bend your elbows slightly.

Focus Points

- Keep your arms extended, and flex your elbows when pressing in.
- Keep your head up so that your eyes remain above the surface.
- Move your arms quickly.

Tips

- Using a pull buoy between your legs may help.
- For an advanced variation, try going backward (feet first).

Purpose

To practice combining sculling and kicking.

Procedure

Repeat drill 37 (Front Scull), but add a flutter kick.

Focus Points

- Keep your arms extended in front of you, sweeping out and pressing in (a).
- Keep your head up so that your eyes remain above the surface.
- Move your arms quickly (b).

Tip

For an advanced variation, do this drill backward or staying in place.

Purpose

To practice the pulling action of the freestyle and backstroke.

Procedure

1. Position your body on its side.
2. The top arm will not be used and should stay down at your side. Stretch your bottom arm out ahead of you.
3. Begin sculling, using a variety of actions—sideways, downward, and so on. Keep the hand action fast (a, b).
4. Keep your hand above the level of your shoulder.

Focus Points

- Move your hand quickly.
- Keep your body steady.

Tips

- Using a pull buoy between your legs may help.
- Try to combine the action of this drill with kicking.

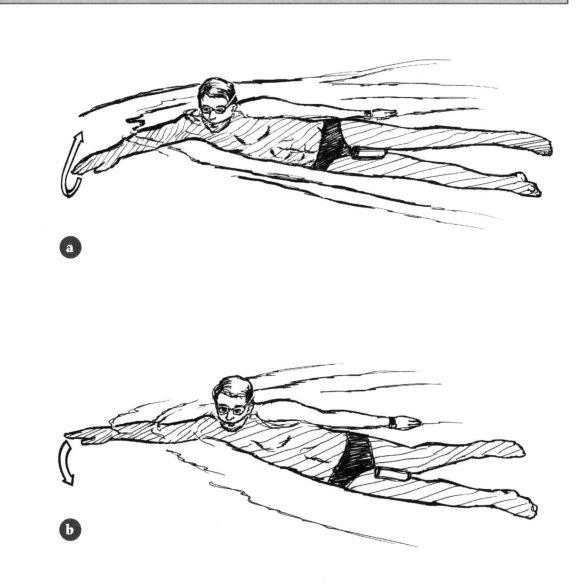

chapter 4

Backstroke

Backstroke is the only competitive stroke performed on the back. Executing it well requires not only sound technical skills but also a high degree of comfort while swimming on the back. In addition, swimmers must practice safely to prevent injury.

The best backstrokers

- maintain excellent body position with the hips and torso up high;
- have a smooth, relaxed stroke recovery with the arms entering directly in line with the shoulders;
- have excellent head control, keeping the head steady;
- have good hip rotation, torso rolling, and shoulder lift;
- have flawless kicking; and
- pull through the water efficiently and with great power.

The drills presented in this chapter will help swimmers improve all of these fundamental aspects of their backstrokes.

Purpose

To isolate and emphasize the arm action of the backstroke recovery.

Procedure

1. Stand next to a wall that is taller than you are when your arms are stretched above your head.

2. Position your body with your side to the wall so that your shoulder is 1 or 2 inches from the wall (a). You will be using just the arm next to the wall. Keep that arm close to the wall at all times during this drill.

3. Start with your arm straight and palm against your thigh. Keeping your arm straight, lift it up as if you were to shake hands with an imaginary person in front of you (b).

4. Rotate your arm inward at the shoulder, keeping the elbow straight and turning your palm down. By the time your hand is as high as your head, your palm should be facing down on top of an imaginary person's head.

5. Continue to rotate your palm as you lift your arm until the arm is directly overhead. When your arm is straight up, the palm should be facing the wall (c). Repeat this movement several times. Begin slowly, and gradually build up speed.

Focus Points

- Imagine painting a large arc with your fingers as you do this drill.
- Perform this drill slowly and with great control.
- Stay close to the wall.

Tip

Practice at home in front of a mirror. Watch to see that your arms recover directly above your shoulders.

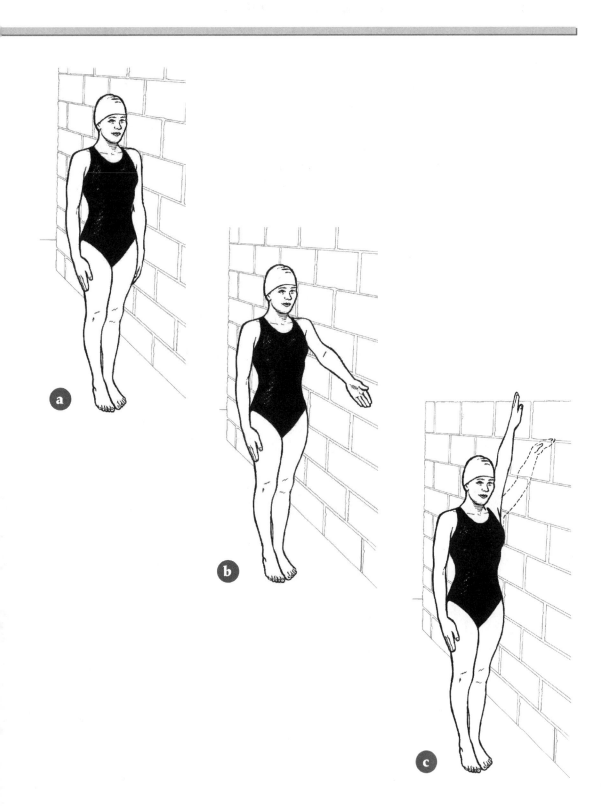

Purpose

To practice full-speed backstroke kicking while maintaining correct body position.

Procedure

1. Repeat drill 15 (Streamline Back Flutter Kick). However, put on fins for more power. Hold a good streamline and correct body position *(a, b)*.
2. Begin to kick more forcefully and quickly.

Focus Points

- Remember: float, streamline, kick.
- Keep your hands just under the water.
- Keep your toes pointed and ankles relaxed.
- Boil the water, but do not splash.
- Keep your head back so that your ears are under the water and cradled by the arms.
- Keep your abdomen up—feel the bottom of your rib cage up on the surface.

Tip

See how hard you can kick so as to boil the water as much as possible. Have a boiling contest with a friend! Remember to boil, not splash.

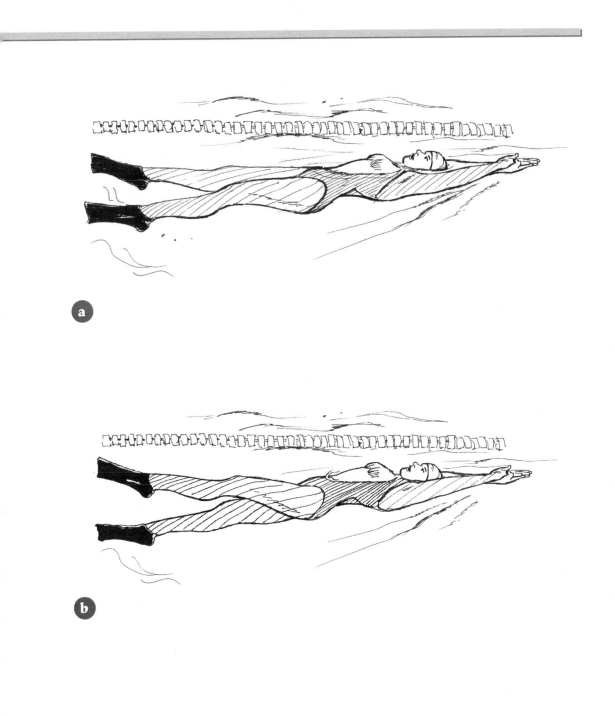

Purpose

This drill is an intermediate step to help move into the correct backstroke position.

Procedure

1. Put on fins. Begin by pushing off the wall on your back with just one arm above your head in a half-streamline position.
2. Position your extended arm with the palm facing up and the thumb in. Straighten your elbow. Extend your arm forward from the shoulder, close to but not quite touching the head. Keep your other arm down at your side.
3. Use a flutter kick to move along the surface. Keep the bottom of your rib cage up and your head steady (a, b).

Focus Points

- Keep the head stationary. Keep the ears level, just below the surface.
- Keep your shoulders steady.
- Control the position of your hand above your head so that the palm faces up.

Tip

Balance a cup on top of your chest, right at the bottom of your sternum.

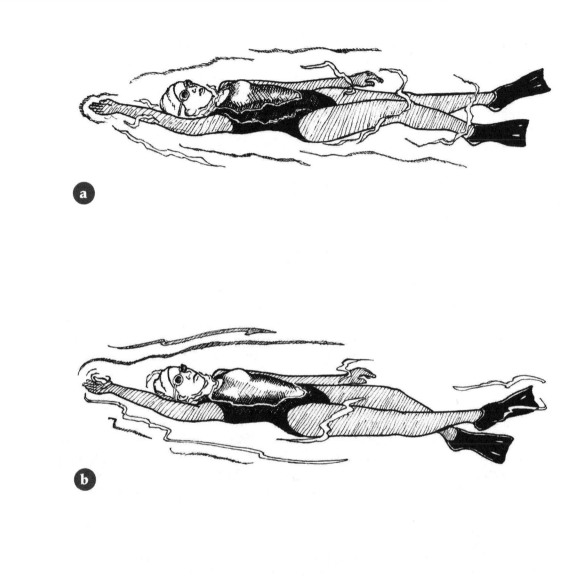

a

b

Purpose

When we study how the body moves most effectively through the water during backstroke or freestyle, we notice that the best swimmers have a certain degree of rotation in the long axis and that their bodies stay high in relation to the surface of the water. Here's the logic of how this works, with a very simple explanation.

In chapter 1, you saw that the body has a natural buoyancy and that some people have better buoyancy than others. The best swimmers move through the water with most of the body below the surface, but a good deal of the body is above, too. Humans are not designed to move through the water as fish do; we do not move completely underwater with our bodies in a vertical position. And, we are not flat as rafts are, either. The closest model that represents the human body's natural buoyancy is that of a sailboat. If you have ever sailed a good-sized sailboat, you'll probably recognize what I mean.

Much of the sailboat is actually underwater. As it moves through the water, an interesting thing happens when the sails catch the wind just right—the boat lifts and cuts through the water even more easily. This usually happens when the boat is at more of an angle. It's really fun to notice when it happens! Swimmers can shape their body position for freestyle and backstroke the same way—at an angle that gives the body more lift, less drag, and greater speed!

Procedure

When you are providing propulsion from a flutter kick, you can position your body on an angle to imitate a sailboat and get an additional lift. For most, this angle is about 45 degrees, yet it can vary from one individual to another. The key is to feel the body lift to the highest position possible while moving through the water. The higher the body position, the less drag. The less drag, the easier it is to move through the water. And the easier it is to move through the water, the faster you swim!

Focus Points

- When on your back, keep your head position straight. Focus on feeling the shoulder, elbow, and side of the rib cage all on the same side at the surface.
- When on your front, keep your head position straight with the nose down.

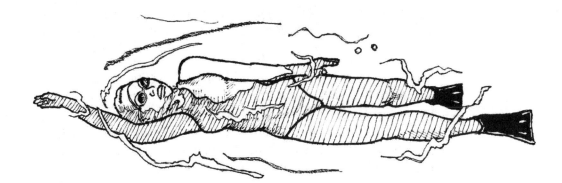

Purpose

To establish the sailboat phase of the backstroke, with control of the body and hand positions. This drill is the most important of the backstroke series.

Procedure

1. Put on fins. Begin by pushing off as you did in drill 42 (One-Arm Extended Back Kick), with one arm extended.
2. Rotate the extended arm deeper in the water, and move the body to the sailboat angle as you continue kicking. When your body is in the sailboat angle, you should feel the shoulder, elbow, and side of the rib cage on the other side all being at the surface.
3. Rotate the extended arm so that the palm is vertical, with the pinky down and the thumb up. The arm should be 6 to 10 inches below the surface.

Focus Points

- Keep the head stationary and in a straight alignment. Keep the ears level, just below the surface.
- Feel the shoulder, elbow, and side of the rib cage all on the same side at the surface.
- Keep the wrist of the extended arm very straight.

Tips

- For the hand position, think of the thumb as a periscope and make sure you keep the periscope in position to come up.
- For an advanced version, use a FINIS Freestyler Hand Paddle on the extended arm. I like this hand paddle because of the skeg, which allows the swimmer to feel the correct alignment. No other hand paddle has this feature.
- Try this drill with your eyes closed, and see if you move in a straight line.
- Try balancing a cup on your forehead while you do this drill.

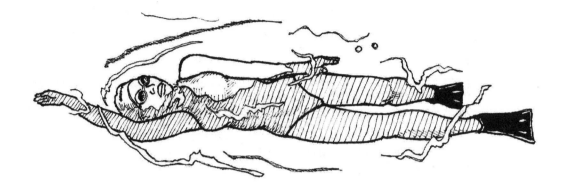

Purpose
To isolate and emphasize the shoulder rotation action of the backstroke.

Procedure
1. Because this drill requires strong kicking, put on fins.
2. Begin by floating on your back and flutter kicking with your arms down at your sides. Keeping the head position steady, slowly begin to roll one shoulder up and into the sailboat angle on one side.
3. Pause at the sailboat angle so that you can feel the shoulder, elbow, and side of the rib cage up at the surface on that side (a). Hold the position for a count of three.
4. Slowly begin to roll your body to the other side (b). You should feel your rib cage up at the surface the whole time you are rolling across to the other side.
5. Continue repeating the motion, rolling from one side to the other and back again. Once you pass the backstroke flags at the other end of the pool, put one arm up above your head so that you can finish safely at the wall. (The flags on either end of the pool, called backstroke flags, are there to help you turn or finish properly.)

Focus Points
- Keep your head steady.
- Roll slowly. It is not important how fast you do this drill, only how well you do it!
- Keep the kicking quick and constant.
- Roll your body from the sailboat angle on one side to the other side. Keep the rib cage up.

Tip
For an advanced version, get into deep water, and position your body vertically. From the deck, have someone place his or her hands on both sides of your head and hold you just above the surface. Then, work on rolling your shoulders back and forth. This creates a washing machine action.

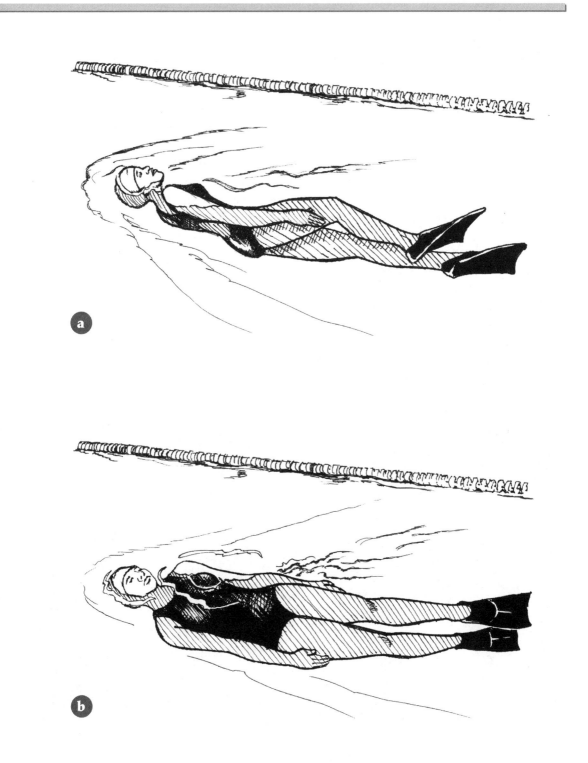

Purpose

To emphasize the beginning of the recovery phase of the backstroke.

Procedure

1. Begin as you did drill 45 (Shoulder Roll Drill) *(a)*.
2. Once you have rolled your body to one side, hold the sailboat angle, lift the arm on the same side as the shoulder that is up *(b)*.
3. Keeping the elbow and wrist straight, and with the thumb up and the pinky down, slowly lift the arm just a few inches above the surface of the water. Then, slowly lower the arm back to your side.
4. Roll to the other side, and repeat *(c, d)*.

Focus Points

- Keep your head steady.
- Roll slowly, then lift.
- Kick hard as you lift your arm slowly so that your body can stay up.

Tip

Look down the top of your arm as you lift. Be sure that your arm is pointing straight.

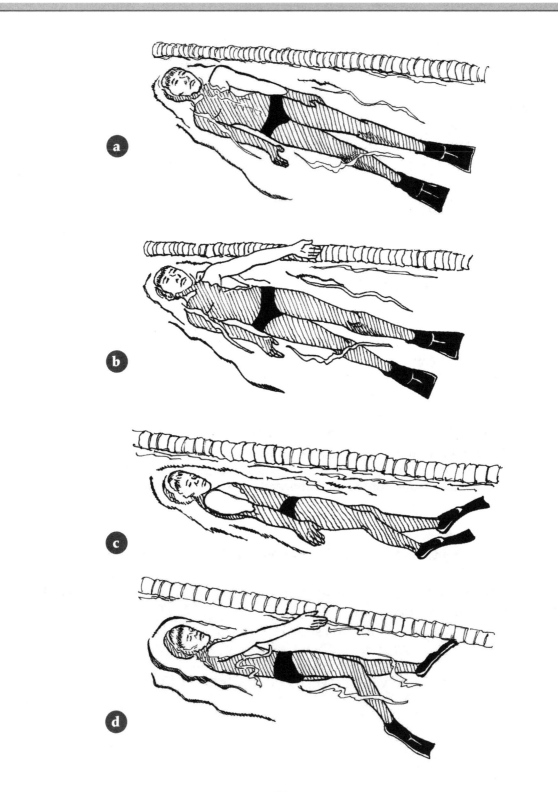

Purpose

To emphasize the backstroke pulling action in combination with the recovery and rolling actions.

Procedure

1. Put on fins.
2. Start by flutter kicking in a lateral backstroke kicking position with the extended arm right next to the lane rope and your body in the sailboat angle (a). Hold this position for a count of three. You will use only the extended arm that is next to the lane rope; the other arm will stay down at your side.
3. Grab the lane rope. Gently pull your body along the rope (b), completing the pull down at your thigh.
4. As you complete the pull, roll the shoulder of the pulling arm up so that you are in the sailboat angle on the other side (c). Hold this position for a count of three while you continue kicking.
5. Slowly recover the pulling arm by lifting it through the air (d). Your hand travels in a large arc until it enters the water overhead. Rotate your arm during the recovery so that your thumb comes out of the water first and your pinky enters the water first. Your hand should enter the water next to the lane rope, with the "periscope" thumb up.
6. As your hand enters the water, roll the opposite shoulder up into the sailboat angle. This completes one cycle.
7. Continue to repeat this cycle. Be sure to keep your arm extended in the water above your head when you pass the flags so that you finish safely at the wall. You should follow this pattern: 1, 2, 3, pull, roll, 4, 5, 6, recover, roll.

Focus Points

- You should roll back and forth into the sailboat angle from one side to the other.
- Stay very close to the lane rope.
- Perform the drill slowly.
- Keep the kicking quick and strong.

Tip

Recite this pattern to yourself as you do the drill: 1, 2, 3, pull, roll, 4, 5, 6, recover, roll.

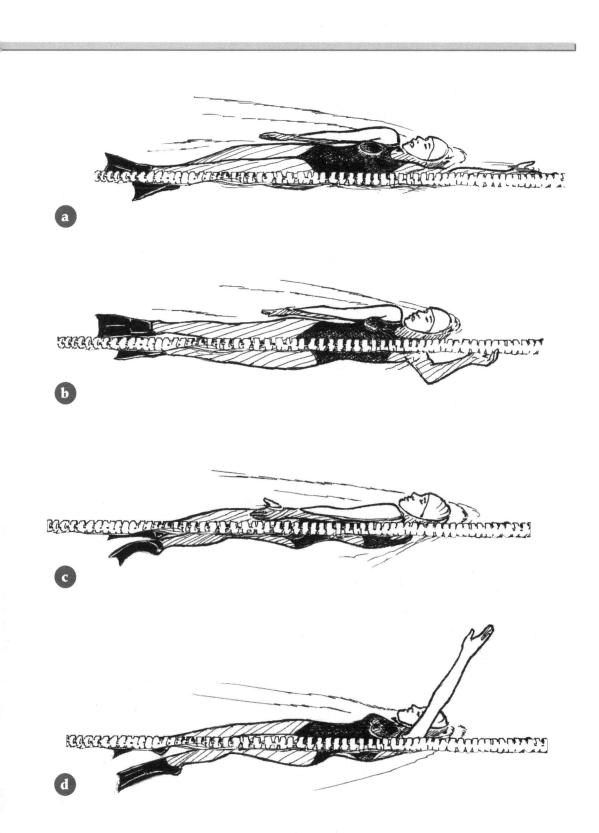

Purpose

To develop the complete backstroke action with control. This is another key drill in the backstroke series.

Procedure

Perform this drill exactly as the previous drill, except don't use the lane rope for pulling. The pulling action will be along an imaginary lane rope that is about 1 foot deep.

1. Put fins on.
2. Start by kicking in a lateral backstroke kicking position right next to the real lane rope with the extended arm next to the rope (*a*). Hold this position for a count of three. You will use only the arm that is extended next to the lane rope; the other arm will stay down at your side.
3. Pull under the lane rope along an imaginary lane rope (*b*), and complete the pull down at your thigh.
4. As you complete the pull, roll the shoulder of the pulling arm up, well above the surface (*c*). Hold this position for a count of three while you continue kicking.
5. Slowly recover the pulling arm (*d*). Your hand should enter the water next to the lane rope, with the "periscope" thumb up.
6. As your hand enters the water, roll the opposite shoulder up. This completes one cycle.
7. Continue to repeat this cycle. Be sure to keep your arm extended above your head when you pass the flags so that you finish safely at the wall. Remember this pattern: 1, 2, 3, pull, roll, 4, 5, 6, recover, roll.

Focus Points

- You should roll from the sailboat angle on one side to the other.
- Stay within 2 inches of the lane rope.
- Keep the kicking quick and strong.

Tip

Recite this cycle to yourself as you do the drill: 1, 2, 3, pull, roll, 4, 5, 6, recover, roll.

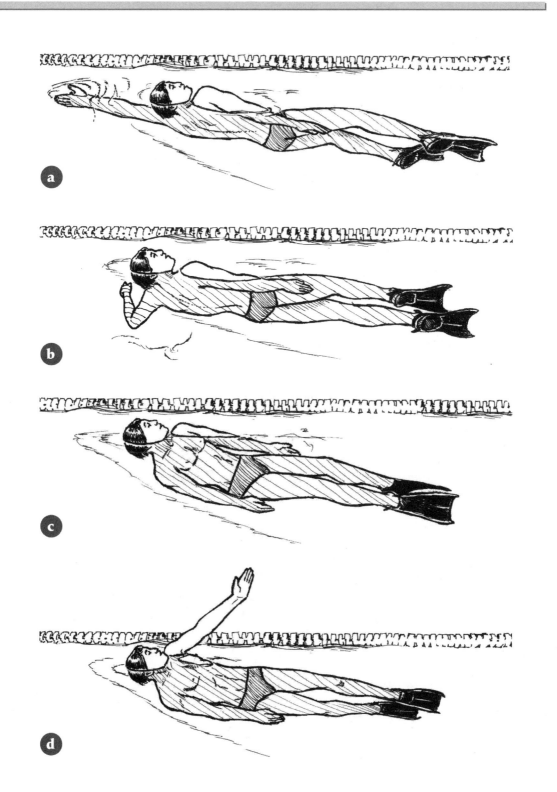

Purpose
To encourage the development of bent-elbow backstroke pulling.

Procedure
1. Put on fins. Begin by flutter kicking on your back with both arms down at your sides *(a)*. Hold this position for a count of three.
2. Recover both arms at the same time *(b)*. Once the hands enter the water, hold this position, with your arms stretched overhead and your hands barely underwater, for a count of three *(c)*.
3. Pull both arms at the same time, and finish at your side *(d)*. This completes one cycle.
4. Continue to repeat this cycle. Be sure to keep your arms above your head when you pass the flags so that you finish safely at the wall.

Focus Points
- Keep your body position steady. Avoid any bouncing.
- Perform the drill slowly.
- Keep the kicking quick and strong.

Tips
- Think of pulling on imaginary lane ropes that are very close to either side of you.
- For an advanced version, perform this drill with a pull buoy between your legs while keeping your body position very steady.

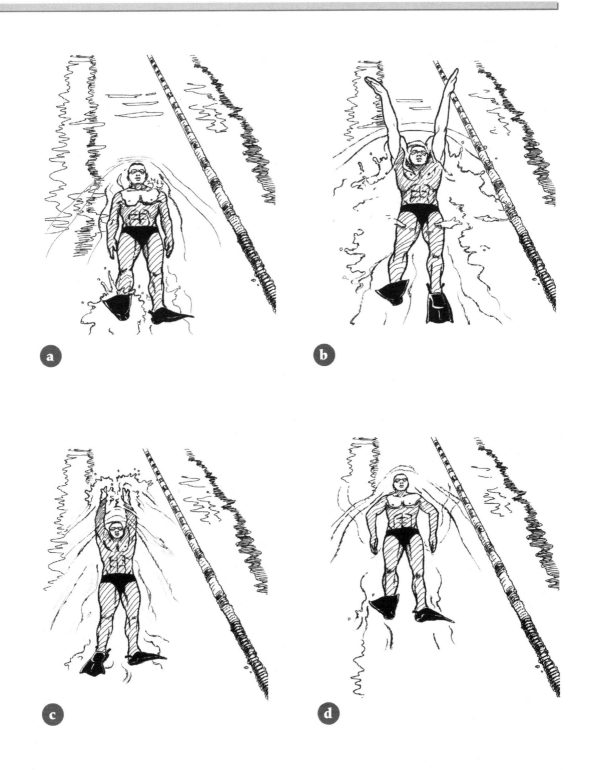

Purpose

To develop the complete backstroke action with control and coordination of both arms. This is another key drill in the backstroke series.

Procedure

This drill is the same as drill 48 (Controlled One-Arm Backstroke), except that in this drill you will use both arms.

1. Put on fins. Start by kicking in a lateral backstroke kicking position with the right arm extended and the left arm down at your side (a). Hold this position for a count of three.
2. Switch arms at the same time by pulling with the right arm and recovering with the left arm (b) until you reach the lateral backstroke kicking position with the left arm up and right arm down (c). Hold this position for a count of three.
3. Repeat the switch. This completes one stroke cycle.
4. Continue to repeat this cycle. Be sure to keep your arm extended above your head when you pass the flags so that you finish safely at the wall.

Focus Points

- Roll from one side to the other.
- Perform the drill slowly and smoothly.
- Keep the kicking quick and strong.

Tip

Switch both arms at the same time. Imagine a teeter-totter—let your shoulders rock back and forth with that motion. Let the shoulders lead the way. Rotate first the shoulders, then the arms.

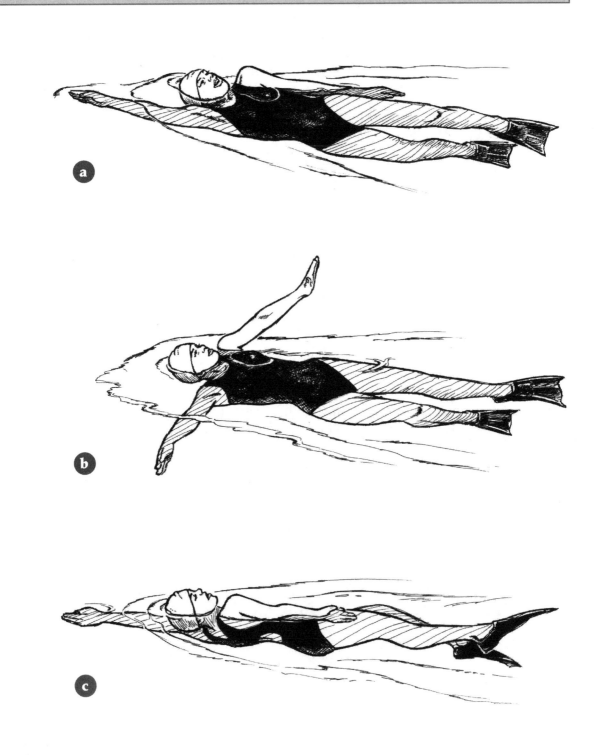

51   CONTINUOUS ONE-ARM BACKSTROKE

Purpose

To emphasize stroke control and body roll with the focus on just one arm. This is the fourth key drill in the backstroke series.

Procedure

Perform this drill exactly like drill 48 (Controlled One-Arm Backstroke) but without pausing between strokes.

1. Put on fins. Start in a lateral backstroke kicking position (a). You will use the arm extended above your head, and the other arm will stay down at your side.
2. Using a continuous action, pull and recover one arm (b-d). Concentrate on excellent shoulder and body roll and a steady head position.
3. Keep one arm above your head when you pass the flags so that you finish safely at the wall.

Focus Points

- Keep rolling from one side to the other.
- Perform the stroke smoothly. Do not pause at any point in the stroke.
- Keep the kicking quick and strong.

Tip

Watch your shoulders, and rotate each one into the sailboat angle each time. Remember to imagine that teeter-totter movement.

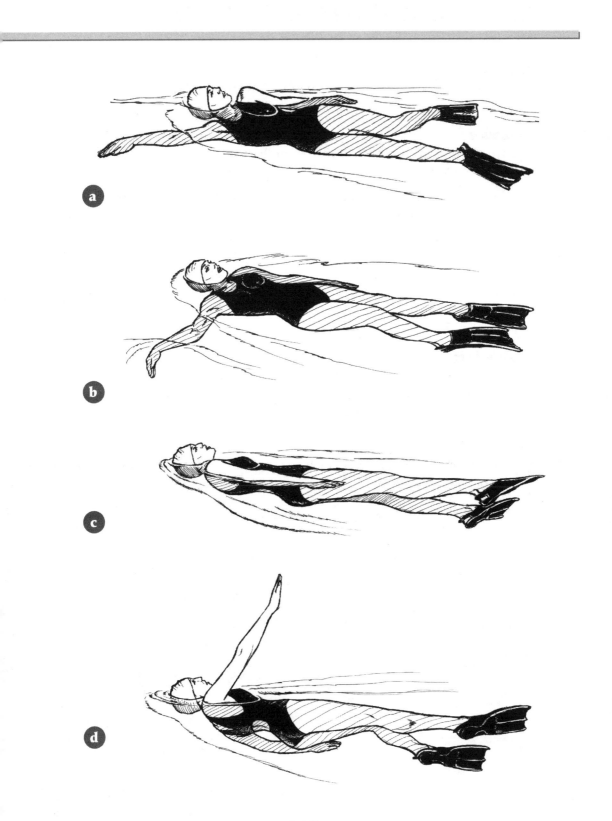

Purpose

To emphasize stroke control and body roll with the coordination of using both arms.

Procedure

Perform this drill exactly as drill 48 (Controlled One-Arm Backstroke), but use both arms at the same time.

1. Put on fins. Start by kicking in a lateral backstroke kicking position.
2. Using a smooth, continuous action, switch both arms at the same time (*a*).
3. Let the shoulders lead the arm action. Lift the shoulders to the sailboat angle on the recovery. Do not pause at any point in the stroke.
4. Continue to repeat the cycle. Be sure to place one arm into the water extended above your head when you pass the flags so that you finish safely at the wall (*b*).

Focus Points

- Keep rolling back and forth from one side to the other.
- Perform the stroke smoothly. Do not pause at any point in the stroke.
- Keep the kicking quick and strong.

Tip

Watch your shoulders, and rotate each one out to the sailboat angle. Remember to imagine that teeter-totter movement.

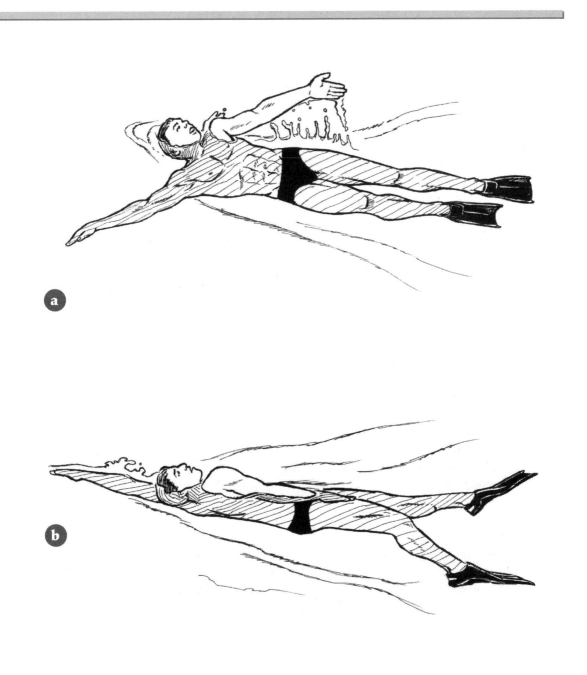

Purpose

To practice the backstroke, focusing particularly on correct position of the hands as they enter the water. Now that you have excellent shoulder and body roll in the backstroke, you will be able to swim the stroke with what feels like a wider stroke.

Procedure

1. For most swimmers, the hands should feel like they are entering the water at the 10 o'clock and 2 o'clock positions. This will feel deceptively easy, and if the stroke is correct, it should.

2. Swim a smooth, controlled backstroke (a, b), concentrating on feeling your hands enter the water at the 10 and 2 positions. You may also notice that the stroke will move a little quicker. This is okay. Be sure you keep the good shoulder roll, steady body position, and strong kicking.

3. Have your coach or training partner stand on the deck at the end of your lane to see if your hands enter the water right above your shoulders. Do not over- or underreach. The most common problem is overreaching (when the hands enter past the line of the respective shoulder; for example, if the hand enters directly over the head.) Make adjustments as necessary.

Focus Points

- Make sure your hands feel as if they enter the water at 10 o'clock and 2 o'clock.
- Don't forget to maintain all of the correct mechanics of the backstroke: steady body position, quick and strong kicking, and a good shoulder roll.

Tip

Swimming next to the lane rope is another way to check your arm entry position. Your hand should enter the water right next to the lane rope. Also, while swimming next to the lane rope, perform a few strokes with your eyes closed to help you really feel the stroke.

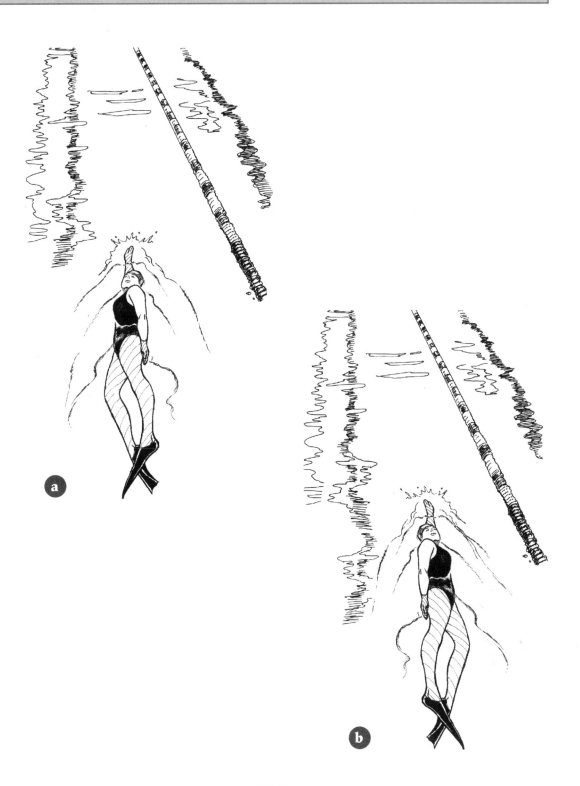

chapter 5

Freestyle

Freestyle is the fastest of the competitive strokes. However, in competition swimmers often try to speed up their time by moving their arms faster through the air, trying so hard that their strokes actually deteriorate and slow them down. To move faster, swimmers must balance good technique with strong pulling and kicking.

The best freestylers

- maintain excellent head and body position with their bodies high out of the water;
- have a smooth, relaxed stroke recovery with the elbows high and hands traveling close to the body;
- have excellent head control;
- breathe comfortably;
- have good hip rotation, torso rolling, and shoulder lift;
- have flawless kicking; and
- pull through the water efficiently and with great power.

The drills in this chapter will help swimmers apply these characteristics of the best freestylers to their own strokes.

Purpose

To practice full-speed freestyle kicking while maintaining a flat body position.

Procedure

1. Start at the wall with fins on.
2. Take a deep breath, push off the wall, and place your hands in a streamline position—nose down, with the hands, shoulders, hips, and heels at the surface (a).
3. Slide for a couple of seconds, then start kicking with a quick, steady flutter kick (b). Keep your toes in the water at all times. The heels of your feet should just barely break the surface of the water. Your hips should be right at the surface.
4. Keep your head tucked in under your arms. Slowly let your air out and go about halfway across the pool, then stop. Repeat.

Focus Points

- Keep your arms in the streamline position.
- Kick the water, not the air. In other words, avoid lifting your feet above the surface of the water. While the splashing may look impressive, it does nothing!
- Keep your hips up.

Tips

- Try to position your head so that it is just barely breaking the surface or is slightly below the surface. This will help get you ready for the freestyle drills.
- Do this drill with the FINIS Snorkel.

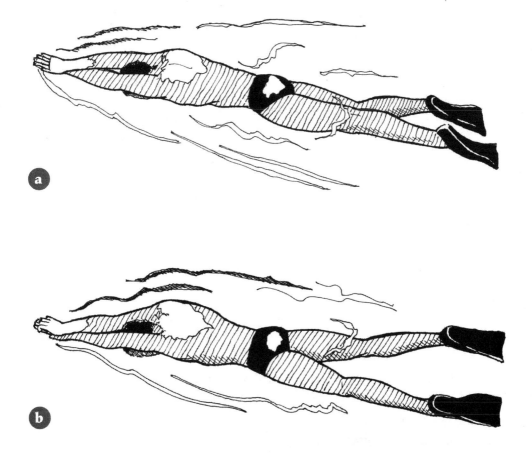

a

b

Purpose

This drill is an intermediate step to help transition into the lateral freestyle kicking position.

Procedure

1. Put fins on. Begin by pushing off the wall on your front with just one arm extended in a half-streamline position *(a)*.
2. Your extended arm should be positioned with the palm facing down. Your elbow should be straight and your arm should be extended forward from the shoulder, close to but not quite touching the head.
3. Keep your other arm down at your side.
4. Use a flutter kick and move along the surface *(b)*. Keep your shoulders and hips up.
5. Keep your head steady.
6. Slowly let out your air as you go about halfway across the pool, and then stop. Repeat.

Focus Points

- The head should remain stationary. Keep the ears level and just below the surface.
- Keep your shoulders steady.
- Control the position of your hand that is extended so the palm faces down.

Tip

Do this drill with the FINIS Snorkel.

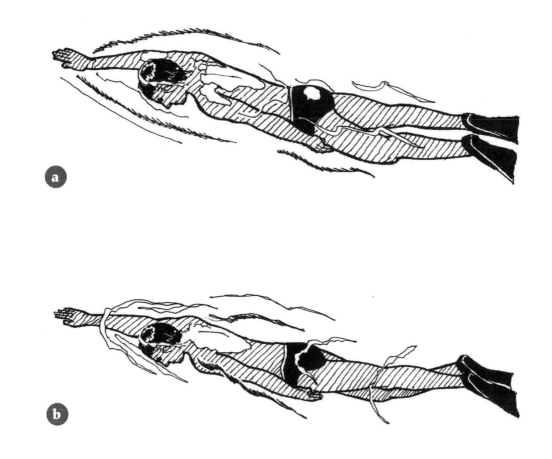

Purpose

To establish the sailboat phase of the freestyle, with control of the body and hand positions. This is the most important key drill of the freestyle series.

Procedure

1. Review the sailboat angle discussion in drill 43 (The Sailboat Angle). You will be focusing on getting into the sailboat angle while on your front side.
2. Put on fins. Start by pushing off on your front, with one arm extended and begin flutter kicking (*a*).
3. Rotate the extended arm deeper in the water, and move the body to the sailboat angle as you continue kicking. You should feel the shoulder, elbow, and the side of the hip on the other side all being at the surface. This is the sailboat angle.
4. Rotate the extended arm so that the palm is horizontal, facing down. The arm should be 6 to 10 inches below the surface (*b*).
5. Look straight down at the bottom of the pool, with just the back of the head breaking the surface.
6. With a steady kick, go halfway across the pool without a breath. Stop, and repeat.

Focus Points

- Keep the head stationary and in straight alignment.
- Feel the shoulder, elbow, and side of the hip all on the same side at the surface.
- Keep the wrist of the extended arm very straight.

Tips

- For an advanced version, use a FINIS Freestyler Hand Paddle on the extended arm—my favorite!
- Kick with your body right over the black line without letting the extended arm move across the line.
- Try this drill with your eyes closed, and see if you move in a straight line.
- Also try this with the FINIS Snorkel.

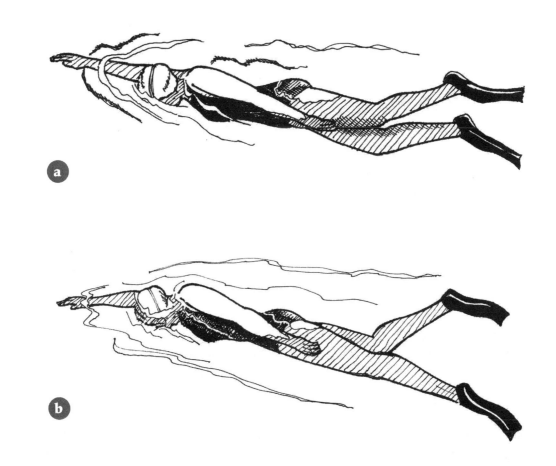

Purpose

To add the breathing action of the freestyle and to continue to practice control of the body position and head position. This is another key drill in the freestyle series.

Procedure

1. Put on fins. Push off the wall into the position described in drill 56 (Lateral Freestyle Kick). Hold the sailboat angle steady throughout this drill.
2. Begin kicking while looking down at the bottom with the back of your head just barely above the surface (a). Hold this position for a count of three. Be sure to blow a steady stream of bubbles.
3. Rotate your head to turn away from the extended arm. Turn the head enough so that your mouth is at the surface and you can sneak a breath in (b). Inhale.
4. Rotate your head back down so that you are looking straight down again. Begin to blow bubbles as soon as your face reenters the water.
5. Continue to repeat the cycle.

Focus Points

- When your face is in the water, look straight down.
- Rotate at the neck to breathe. Keep the crown of your head in one spot—rotate the head, don't lift it.
- Keep your body in the sailboat angle. Feel your shoulder, elbow, and hip up at all times.

Tips

- Practice this drill on both sides so that you will learn to be comfortable with alternate breathing.
- Use a FINIS Freestyler Hand Paddle on the extended arm to help you get the feel of keeping your body on keel while you breathe.

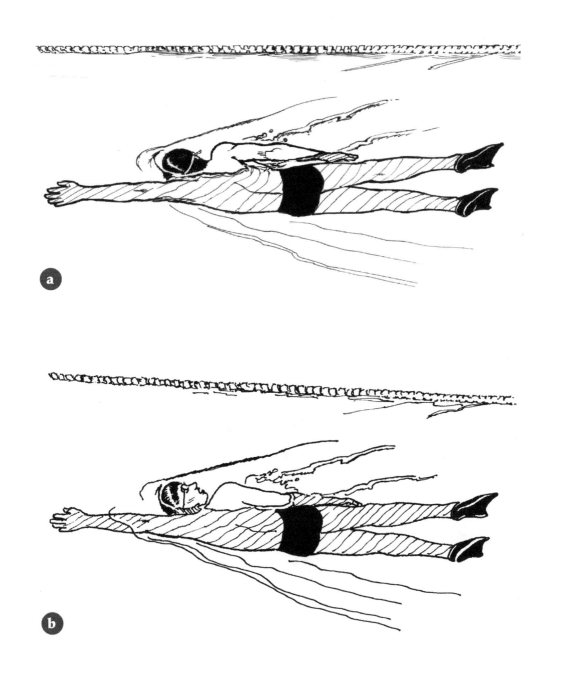

Purpose

To emphasize the proper mechanics for the arm recovery. This drill is excellent for helping swimmers with chronic shoulder problems retrain their strokes, and usually corrects the problem. Most shoulder pain is caused by improper mechanics, not a deficiency of pain reliever!

Procedure

1. Put on fins. Hold a half-board at the bottom with one arm, and push off. Move your body to the lateral kick position with your head in the breathing position, and kick.

2. Place your other arm down at your side so that the back of your hand is against your thigh (*a*). Then, grab an imaginary zipper between your thumb and forefinger, and pull the zipper up along your body until you reach your armpit (*b*). Allow your wrist to flex.

3. Your thumbnail should stay against your body, pointing toward the middle of your body. Your palm should remain facing up. As you pull up, your wrist should be relaxed and your elbow should come straight up.

4. Once you complete the lifting action, slowly return the arm in the same manner to the starting position. Continue to repeat this cycle. Be sure to practice on both sides.

Focus Points

- Keep the body in the sailboat angle, with your head in the breathing position.
- Perform this drill slowly and with control.
- Lift the elbow straight up as you pull up.

Tip

Try doing this drill while facing a lane rope or high wall. Keep your hand next to your body. This will force you to recover properly.

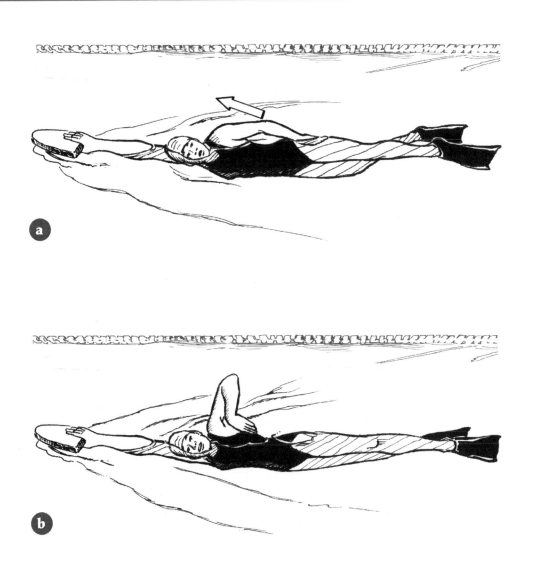

Purpose

To isolate the proper mechanics of the freestyle, one arm at a time. This is another key drill in the freestyle series.

Procedure

1. Put on fins. Hold a half-board with one hand. Place your other hand (which will be pulling) under the board with the knuckles against the board. Start with your eyes looking down and the back of your head just barely above the surface. Your back and hips will be flat on the surface. Kick while you hold this position for a count of three as you blow bubbles (a).

2. After counting to three, begin to pull your arm down and roll your body to the sailboat position (b). As your hand passes under your shoulder, your head should begin turning to the side to breathe.

3. Complete the pull in the stretch position, the same position as in drill 56 (Lateral Freestyle Kick). As you finish the pull, the palm will be facing up (c). Hold this stretched position for an additional count of three.

4. Begin the zip-up action to bring your elbow up. As your hand reaches the middle of your back, begin to return your head to the forward position (d). (The hand should not pass in front of your face on the recovery.)

5. Once the hand reaches the shoulder, rotate the hand forward so that it can slice into the water just in front of the half-board (e). Then, slide the hand under the half-board to complete the cycle (f). Practice with each arm.

6. Repeat this cycle to yourself as you perform the drill: 1, 2, 3, pull, breathe, stretch, 4, 5, 6, elbow, head, hand.

Focus Points

- Keep your head low so that the hips stay up.
- Keep the kicking steady.
- Concentrate on one step at a time.

Tip

For an advanced version, perform this drill next to a lane rope. Use the top of the rope as a guide for your hand when recovering your arm. Let the fingernails of your first and middle fingers gently glide across the top of the lane rope as if it were a piano.

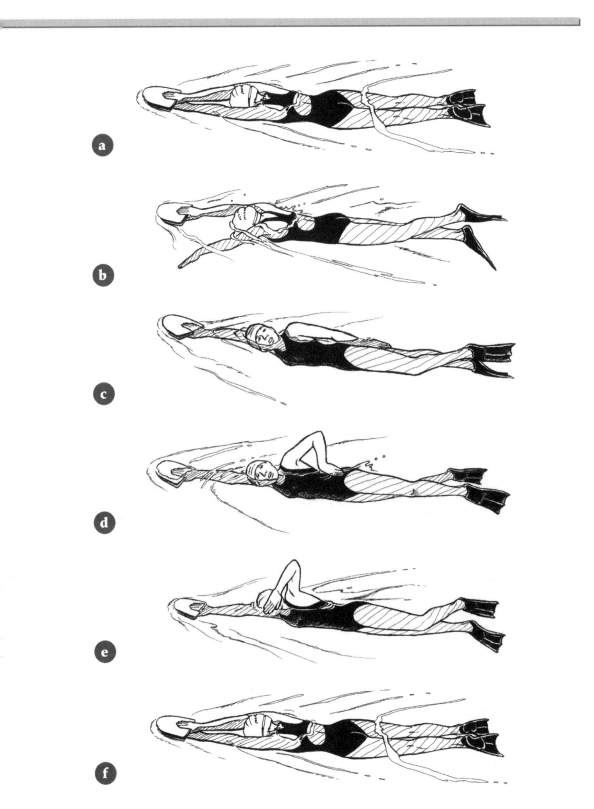

Purpose

To develop the coordinated two-arm freestyle action with control of the timing. This drill will also allow you to feel the complete extension of the freestyle stroke. This is the next key drill in the freestyle series.

Procedure

1. Put on fins. Start by kicking in the position described in drill 56 (Lateral Freestyle Kick), with the left arm extended and the right arm down at your side (a). The shoulder of your right arm will be above the surface. Keep your eyes looking down, and hold your breath. Kick in this position for a count of three.

2. Switch arms at the same time by pulling with the left arm and recovering with the right arm until you reach the position described in drill 56 (Lateral Freestyle Kick), with the right arm up and the left arm down (b-e). Kick in this position for a count of three.

3. Repeat the switch. This completes one stroke cycle. Continue to repeat this cycle.

4. Try to go all the way across the pool without breathing. Use the rhythm of 1, 2, switch, 1, 2, switch.

Focus Points

- Keep your eyes down and hips up.
- Move from the sailboat angle on one side to the sailboat angle on the other side.
- Perform the drill slowly and smoothly.
- Keep the kicking quick and strong.

Tips

- For an advanced version, perform this drill with a FINIS Swimmer's Snorkel. It works great! You can really practice the control of the stroke without having to move the head to breathe.
- You can also add the use of FINIS Freestyler Hand Paddles—one on each hand.

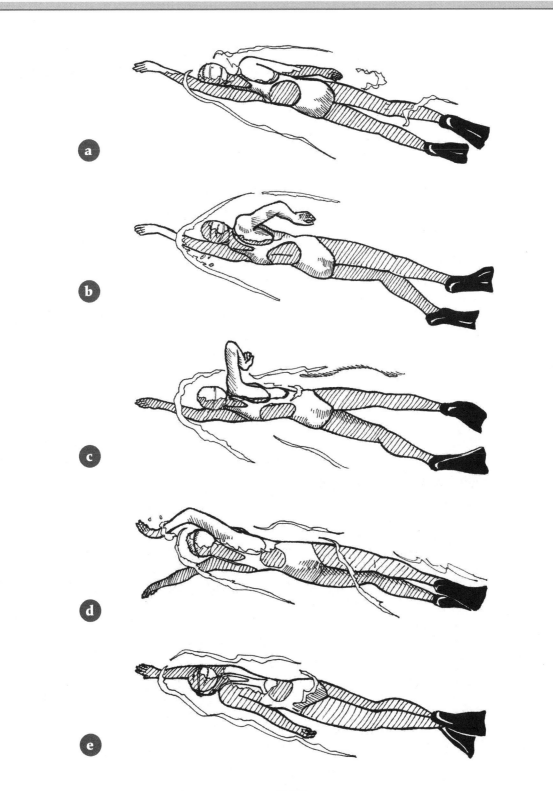

Purpose

To add the dimension of breathing in the freestyle action with control of the timing. This drill will also allow the swimmer to feel the complete extension of the freestyle stroke while breathing. This is the next key drill in the freestyle series.

Procedure

1. Put on fins. Start by kicking in the position described in drill 56 (Lateral Freestyle Kick), with the left arm extended and the right arm down at your side. The shoulder of your right arm will be above the surface. Rotate your head to the breathing position. Kick in this position for a count of three.

2. With a synchronized action of rotating the head through the water all the way to the breathing position on the other side, switch arms at the same time by pulling with the left arm and recovering with the right arm until you reach the Lateral Freestyle Kick position, with the right arm up and the left arm down (a-c). Kick in this position for a count of three.

3. Repeat the switch and head rotation (d-f). This completes one stroke cycle. Continue to repeat this cycle.

4. Use the rhythm of 1, 2, switch & breathe, 1, 2, switch & breathe.

Focus Points

- Move from the sailboat angle on one side to the sailboat angle on the other side.
- Perform the drill slowly and smoothly.
- Rotate the head smoothly, keeping the crown of the head in the water.
- Keep the kicking quick and strong.

Tips

- For an advanced version, perform this drill with your eyes closed for a few strokes, and see if you move in a straight line.
- You can also do this drill with FINIS Freestyler Hand Paddles.

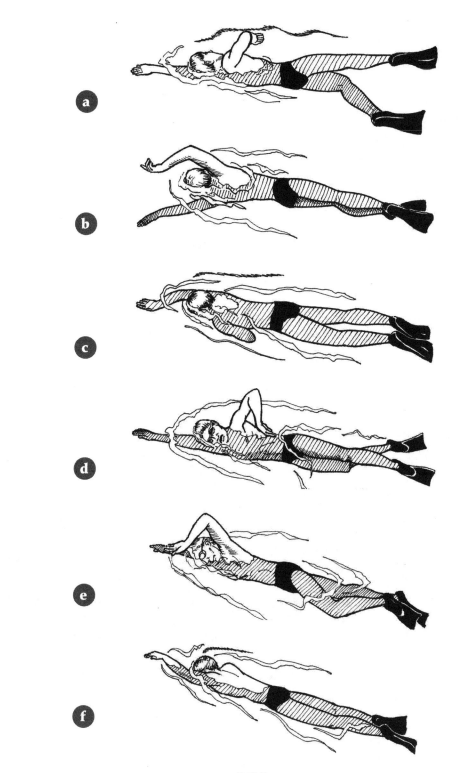

Purpose

To develop the coordinated two-arm freestyle action with control of the timing. This drill will also allow you to feel the complete extension of the freestyle stroke with breathing to one side first. This is the next key drill in the freestyle series.

Procedure

1. Put on fins. Start by kicking in the position described in drill 56 (Lateral Freestyle Kick), with the left arm extended and the right arm down at your side (a). The shoulder of your right arm will be above the surface. Keep your eyes looking down, and remember to blow bubbles. Kick in this position for a count of three.

2. Switch your arms at the same time by pulling with the left arm and recovering with the right arm until you reach the lateral freestyle kick position with the right arm extended and the left arm down (b). As you switch, rotate your head to breathe to your left (c). Kick in this position for a count of three.

3. Repeat the switch (d), and rotate the head so your eyes are down. This completes one stroke cycle. Continue to repeat this cycle for the entire lap.

4. Change to breathing on the other side on the next lap. Get comfortable breathing on either side.

5. The rhythm for this drill is 1, 2, 3, switch & breathe, 1, 2, 3, switch.

Focus Points

- Keep the crown of your head down, and rotate your head when you breathe.
- Move from the sailboat angle on one side to the sailboat angle on the other side.
- Perform the drill slowly and smoothly.
- Keep the kicking quick and strong.

Tips

- Use FINIS Freestyler Hand Paddles. These unique paddles are specifically designed to enhance the freestyle technique. You will get the proper feel for how to move the arm through the water, and also how to recover properly.
- Try a few strokes with your eyes closed, and see if you stay in a straight line.

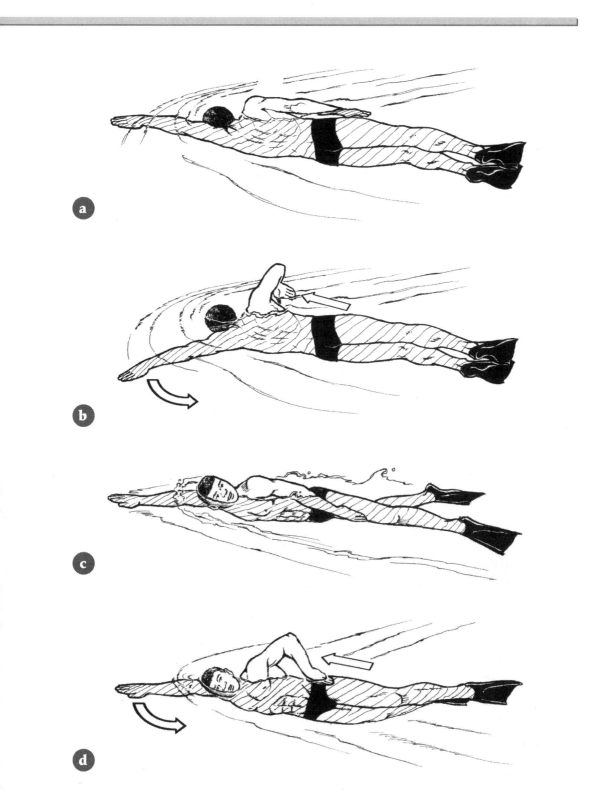

63 CONTROLLED ALTERNATE-BREATHING FREESTYLE

Purpose
To develop alternate breathing with the coordinated two-arm freestyle action. This is the next key drill in the freestyle series. This will be just like the previous drill, except the timing will be a little quicker and the breathing will be every third stroke.

Procedure
1. Put on fins. Start by kicking in the lateral freestyle kick position with the left arm extended and the right arm down at your side. The shoulder of your right arm will be above the surface (a). Keep your eyes looking down, and remember to blow bubbles. Kick in this position for a count of two.
2. Switch your arms at the same time by pulling with the left arm and recovering with the right arm (b, c) until you reach the lateral freestyle kick position with the right arm extended and the left arm down. As you switch, keep your eyes looking down and slowly blow bubbles. Kick in this position for a count of two (d).
3. Switch your arms at the same time by pulling with the right arm and recovering with the left arm until you reach the position described in drill 56 (Lateral Freestyle Kick), with the left arm extended and the right arm down (e). As you switch, rotate your head to breathe to your right. Kick in this position for a count of two.
4. Repeat the switch, and rotate the head so your eyes are down. This completes one stroke cycle. Continue to repeat this cycle for the entire lap, breathing every third stroke.
5. Get comfortable breathing on either side.
6. The rhythm for this drill is 1, 2, switch, 1, 2, switch, 1, 2, switch & breathe.

Focus Points
- Keep the crown of your head down, and rotate your head when you breathe.
- Move from the sailboat angle on one side to the sailboat angle on the other side.
- Perform the drill slowly and smoothly.
- Keep the kicking quick and strong.

Tips
- Use FINIS Freestyler Hand Paddles.
- Try a few strokes with your eyes closed, and see if you stay in a straight line.

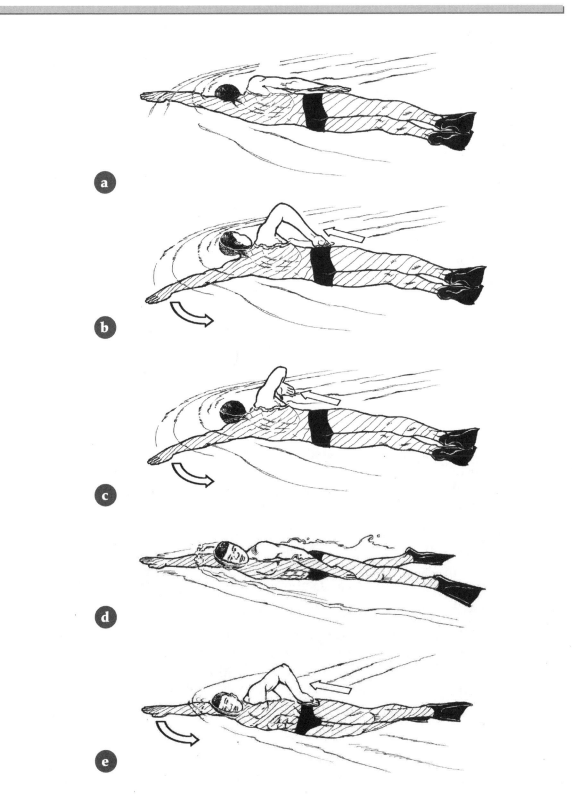

Purpose

To isolate the proper mechanics of the freestyle, one arm at a time. To execute this drill properly, you will need to have excellent kicking and stroke control. This is an advanced drill.

Procedure

The action of this drill is very similar to that of drill 51 (Continuous One-Arm Backstroke). Remember to move your shoulders back and forth continuously from the sailboat angle on one side to the sailboat angle on the other side.

1. Put on fins. Start in the position described in drill 56 (Lateral Freestyle Kick). Use the extended arm in front, and keep the other arm down at your side (a).
2. Using a smooth, continuous action, pull and recover the one arm you are working (b). Concentrate on excellent body roll and good head position control. Reach and pause briefly when the arm is fully extended, and pause briefly when you finish the stroke with your hand down at your side.
3. Breathe on the same side that you are pulling (c). Roll the opposite shoulder so that it completely breaks the surface and reaches the sailboat angle. Keep the hips up.
4. Repeat the action for the other arm.

Focus Points

- Rotate from the sailboat angle on one side to the sailboat angle on the other.
- Keep the hips up as you rotate from one side to the other.
- Perform the stroke slowly and smoothly.
- Get full extension on every stroke. Reach all the way forward, and pull all the way back. It's okay to pause briefly when you stretch and when you finish.
- Keep the kicking quick and strong.

Tips

- Feel the shoulder and upper arm of your down arm come above the surface when you extend the pulling arm forward.
- For an advanced version, try this drill with the FINIS Freestyler Hand Paddle.

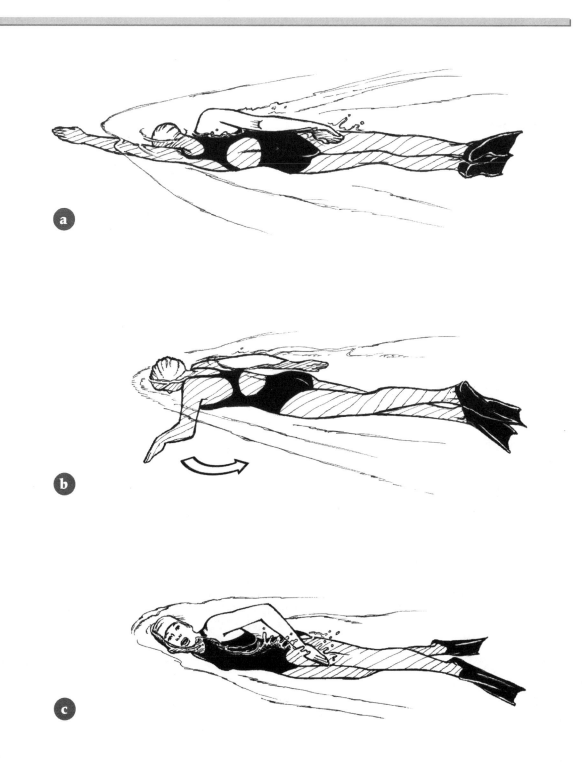

Purpose

To emphasize stroke control and shoulder roll with the coordination of using both arms. This is the final drill in the freestyle series.

Procedure

Perform this drill as drill 64 (Continuous One-Arm Freestyle) but use both arms at the same time.

1. Put on fins. Start by kicking in a one-arm streamline position *(a)*.
2. Using a smooth, continuous action, switch both arms at the same time *(b)*. Pause briefly at the point of full extension in the stroke *(c)*. Be sure to reach full extension and to complete each pull.
3. Continue to repeat the cycle *(d)*. Use alternate breathing.

Focus Points

- Rotate from the sailboat angle on one side to the sailboat angle on the other.
- Keep the hips up as you rotate from one side to the other.
- Perform the stroke slowly and smoothly.
- Get full extension on every stroke. Reach all the way forward, and pull all the way back. It's okay to pause briefly when you stretch and when you finish.
- Keep the kicking quick and strong.

Tips

- Use FINIS Freestyler Hand Paddles.
- Try to slice your hands as they enter the water. Make sure they slice into the water cleanly, and notice whether you have very few air bubbles passing past your face as you swim. The fewer air bubbles, the better.
- Be sure to practice alternate breathing!

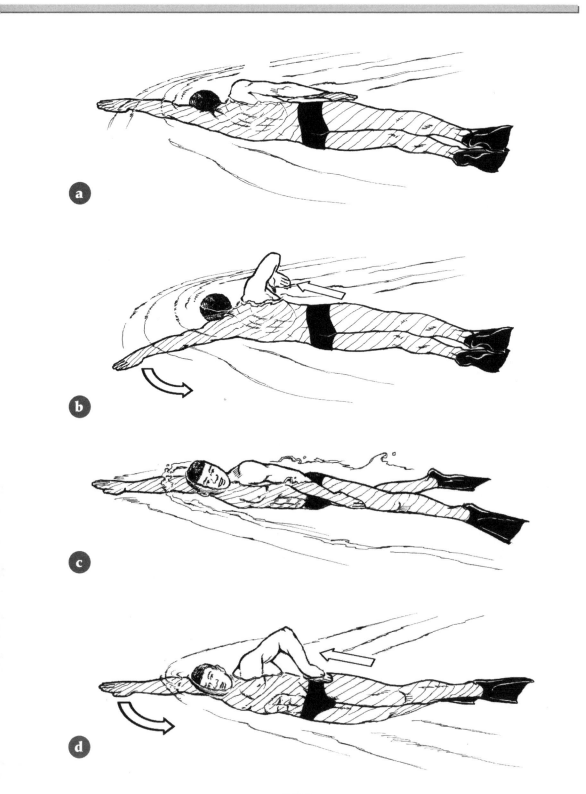

chapter 6

Breaststroke

The breaststroke offers perhaps the greatest variability in style among the strokes. There are almost as many styles of breaststroke as there are breast-stroke coaches. However, some fundamentals are common to almost all great breaststrokers.

The best breaststrokers

- reach an extended position, or glide, at least for an instant on every stroke, assuring full extension and maximum efficiency;
- pull using an outsweep, insweep, and recovery accelerating from the beginning of the pull and not pausing until full extension is reached again;
- keep their hips high throughout the entire stroke;
- complete the kick with a strong squeeze and pointed toes; and
- maintain good head control, always keeping the chin tucked in.

The breaststroke drills in this chapter will teach swimmers these essential techniques for enhancing their strokes. After mastering these fundamentals, they can develop individual variations.

66 STANDING BREASTSTROKE PULLING ACTION

Purpose
To develop the correct mechanics for the breaststroke pull.

Procedure
1. Stand in shallow water so that your shoulders are just above the surface. Position your arms out in front of you so that your thumbs are touching and your palms are facing down and slightly out (*a*). Hold this position for a count of three.
2. Begin the pulling action by sweeping your hands outward just under the surface. You should reach a point where the fingers are still pointing forward (before they begin to point out to the sides) and your hands are apart about the length of one arm (*b*). In essence, you will shape an equilateral triangle; your arms will be the sides and the distance between the hands will be the base.
3. Rotate the hands inward (*c*), begin to bend the elbows back, and sweep your hands in (*d*). Your fingertips will "draw" the sides of the equilateral triangle with the fingertips still facing forward. Sweep in until the fingertips of both hands come together directly in front of and next to your chest (*e*).
4. Shoot the hands forward together, just at or below the surface. Extend your arms completely forward to the starting position (*f*). Repeat the cycle.

Focus Points
- Keep your body standing straight.
- "Draw" the triangle with your fingertips.
- Perform this drill slowly and smoothly at first, then increase your speed.
- Pause only in the starting position.

Tips
- Watch your hands as you perform this drill. You should always see them in front of your shoulders.
- Use FINIS Freestyler Hand Paddles. Focus on keeping the tip of the paddle facing forward at all times as you sweep out and sweep in.

Purpose

To further develop the correct mechanics for the breaststroke pull. This drill also enhances arm pull speed and helps swimmers who tend to overpull or who have a slow arm pull.

Procedure

You will basically do the same arm action as in drill 66 (Standing Breaststroke Pulling Action), but you will now add vertical kicking in deeper water.

1. Put on fins, and move out to deep water. Begin by flutter kicking in a vertical position. Keep your body straight and your head above the surface. Position your arms out in front of you so that your thumbs are touching and your palms are facing down and slightly out (*a*). Hold this position for a count of three.

2. Begin the pulling action by sweeping your hands outward just under the surface (*b*). You should reach a point where the fingers are still pointing forward (before they begin to point out to the sides) and your hands are apart about the length of one arm. In essence, you will shape an equilateral triangle; your arms will be the sides and the distance between the hands will be the base.

3. Rotate the hands inward, begin to bend the elbows back, and sweep your hands in (*c*). Your fingertips will "draw" the sides of the equilateral triangle with the fingertips still facing forward. Sweep in until the fingertips of both hands come together directly in front of and next to your chest (*d*).

4. Next, shoot the hands forward together, just at or below the surface (*e*). Extend your arms completely forward to the starting position. Repeat the cycle.

Focus Points

- Keep your body straight.
- Pause only in the starting position.
- Accelerate and lift as you pull.
- As you sweep your arms in, lift your body higher above the surface, at least to midchest height.
- Shoot your hands forward very quickly.

Tips

- Watch your hands as you perform this drill. You should always see them in front of your shoulders.
- Use FINIS Freestyler Hand Paddles. Focus on keeping the tip of each paddle facing forward at all times as you sweep out and sweep in.

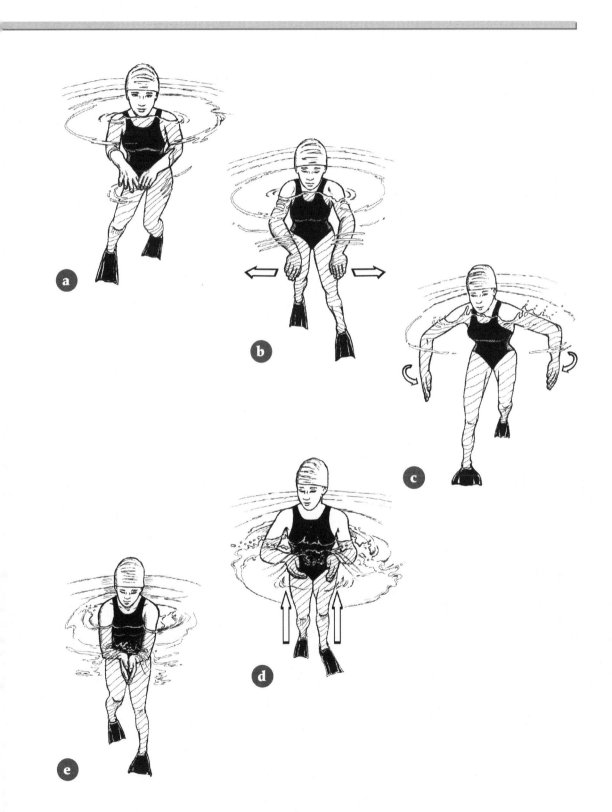

68 BREASTSTROKE PULL AND FLUTTER KICK—HEAD UP

Purpose

To isolate the proper mechanics of the breaststroke pull and to emphasize the necessary speed and lift for the stroke. Keeping the head up permits swimmers to see their arm pull in action and serves as a self-check. It is also more challenging with the head up.

Procedure

1. Put on fins. Kick forward with your arms extended in front of your body, head lifted, with the eyes just above the surface and chin tucked in. Hold your arms extended for a count of three. Then, pull and recover quickly, using the breaststroke arm motion you practiced in the previous two drills *(a)*.
2. Get plenty of lift while pulling. Lift your shoulders higher above the surface, but keep your chin tucked in *(b)*. Return your head to the starting position with the eyes just above the surface. Continue to repeat the cycle *(c)*.
3. The eyes should be just above the surface in the starting position. Keep your chin tucked in while pulling. Look downward at about a 45-degree angle, keeping the head angle steady.

Focus Points

- Be sure to breathe. Blow bubbles when your lower face is in the water to allow you to breathe in quickly when you pull.
- Keep your chin tucked in. Lift the body, not the chin.
- Really stretch and hold the extension for a count of three.

Tips

- When your arms are out in front, you create a "window" that you can look through toward the bottom of the pool. Keep your chin tucked in so that you can always look through the top of the window. Make sure your head angle remains steady.
- For an advanced drill, use FINIS Freestyler Hand Paddles. Focus on keeping the tip of each paddle facing forward at all times as you sweep out and sweep in.

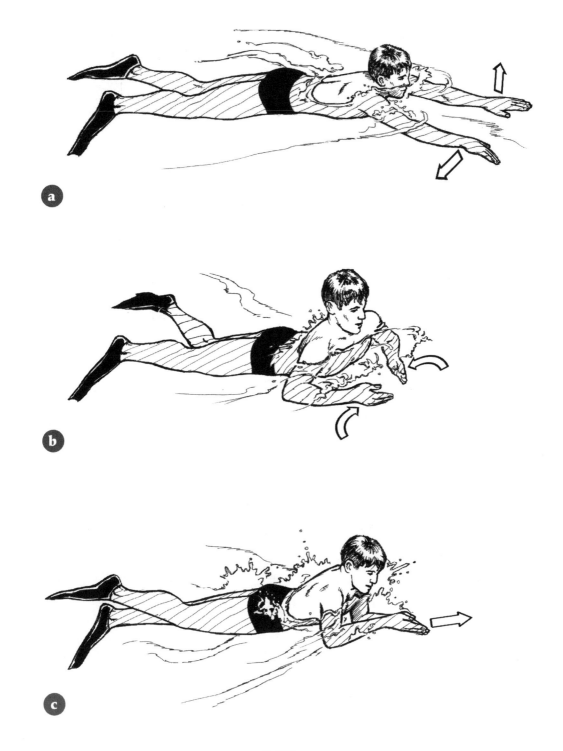

69 BREASTSTROKE PULL AND FLUTTER KICK—HEAD DOWN

Purpose

To isolate the proper mechanics of the breaststroke pull and to emphasize the necessary speed and lift for the stroke while getting the body to as high a buoyancy position as possible. This drill is the same as the previous drill, except you will change your head position to start off in the sliding position.

Procedure

1. Put on fins. Kick forward with your arms extended in front of your body, eyes down, with the back of the head just above the surface and chin tucked in. Hold your arms extended for a count of three. Then, pull and recover quickly, using the breaststroke arm motion you practiced in the previous two drills *(a-c)*.

2. Get plenty of lift while pulling. Lift your shoulders higher above the surface, but keep your nose down and your chin tucked in. Return your head to the starting position with the eyes just above the surface. Continue to repeat the cycle.

3. The eyes should be looking straight down in the starting position. Keep your chin tucked in while pulling. Look downward right into the surface of the water when you pull, and keep the head angle steady.

Focus Points

- Be sure to breathe. Blow bubbles when your face is in the water to allow you to breathe in quickly when you pull.
- Look down, look down, look down! You can still breathe without having to look forward.
- Keep your chin tucked in. Lift the body, not the chin.
- Really stretch and hold the extension for a count of three. Feel your hips come up to the surface when you extend.

Tip

For an advanced drill, use FINIS Freestyler Hand Paddles. Focus on keeping the tip of each paddle facing forward at all times as you sweep out and sweep in.

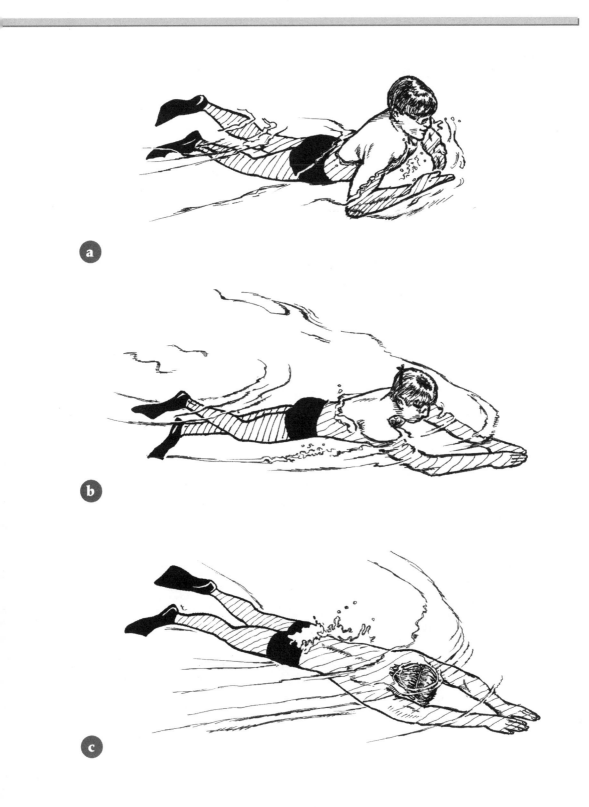

Purpose

To integrate the breathing and kicking phases of the breaststroke while allowing you to feel the slide created in the power phase of the kick. Review the breaststroke kicking drills from chapter 2 before embarking on this drill.

Procedure

1. Hold the bottom edge of a kickboard with the fingers on top and the thumbs wrapped around underneath. Start by pushing off with your nose down and your head barely breaking the surface. Your arms should be completely extended; and your shoulders, hips, and heels should all be at the surface. Point your toes (a).
2. After you push off the wall, hold the slide position for a count of three. Be sure to blow bubbles the whole time your face is in the water.
3. Lift your head up so that your chin is on the surface (b). Your chin should be tucked in and your eyes should be directed downward. Inhale.
4. As you lower your head back into the water, begin your kick by bringing your heels in, then rotate the toes out (c).
5. As your head comes back into position in the water, kick out and squeeze. You will be kicking into the slide position (d).
6. Exhale while your face is back in the water (e). Hold the slide position for a count of three, then repeat the cycle.

Focus Points

- Concentrate on this pattern: breathe, kick, slide.
- Feel how your body slices through the water when you kick and then slide.
- After you finish the slide, lift your head first.
- Feel your hips and heels return to the surface during the slide.

Tips

- Move across the pool with as few kicks as possible, and determine your average number of kicks.
- For a variation, take only one breath for every two or three kicks to help you develop the feel for the slide.
- Try this workout set: Do three 100's kicking, striving for the fewest number of kicks for each 100. It is the best way to develop the power of the breaststroke.

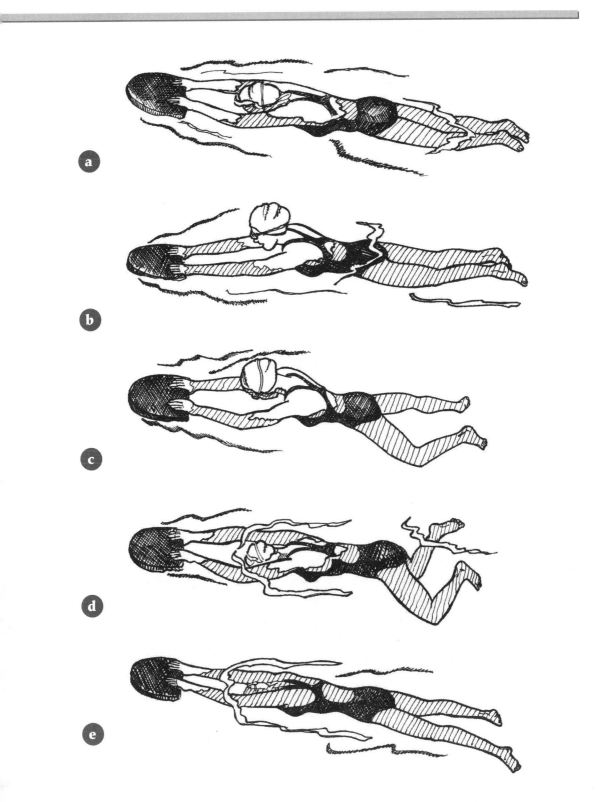

Purpose

To develop the timing for the breaststroke and to emphasize the slide portion of the stroke. This drill is especially useful with new swimmers and with swimmers who have timing issues that need to be corrected.

Procedure

1. Push off the wall with your nose down, in a streamline. Feel your hands, shoulders, hips, and heels at the surface. Take a breath before you push off and then slowly exhale when your face is in the water. Hold the slide for a count of six.
2. Insert one stroke in the middle of two slides. Push off from the wall, and slide for a count of three. Then, use this pattern to do one stroke: pull (*a*), breathe (*b*), kick (*c*), slide. Slide for another count of three, and stop.
3. Practice this drill until the stroke becomes fluid and the slide position is established very quickly after the stroke.

Focus Points

- Be sure to have the nose down on the slide portions.
- Keep your chin tucked in as you lift and breathe.
- Recover your hands high so that you can return to the slide position quickly.

Tips

- Measure the distance you travel when you only slide for a count of six. Make sure that when you add a stroke of breaststroke, you go much farther.
- Make a game of seeing how far you can go with the two slides and one stroke.

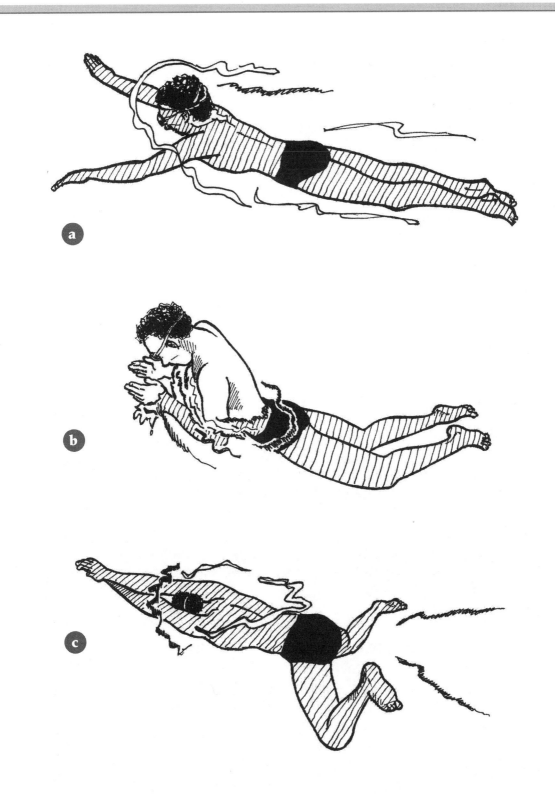

Purpose

To emphasize control along with the proper timing and extension for the breaststroke.

Procedure

1. In this drill, you will simply practice the breaststroke with one pull for each kick and slide, one after another (a-c). Follow this pattern: pull, breathe, kick, slide. Hold each slide for a count of three.
2. Keep your nose down on the slide. On the slide, the back of your head should be at the surface.
3. Count the number of strokes per lap. You should strive for the fewest number of strokes with the three-count slide timing.

Focus Points

- Maintain an even rhythm.
- Hold the slide for a count of three on each stroke.
- Keep the pull quick, and get plenty of lift.
- Control the head and body position.

Tip

To get closer to the timing needed for the racing stroke, gradually reduce the length of time that you hold the glide position. The shorter the race, the quicker the glide; the longer the race, the longer the glide. Here are the glide times to shoot for in races:

- For the 200, hold for a count of two or three.
- For the 100, hold for a count of one or two.
- For the 50, hold for a count of one.

Coaching note: Once the swimmer masters the stroke with consistent head control, the head angle can be modified to allow for optimum body position on the slide. Keep in mind that the breaststroke allows for a lot of individual variation.

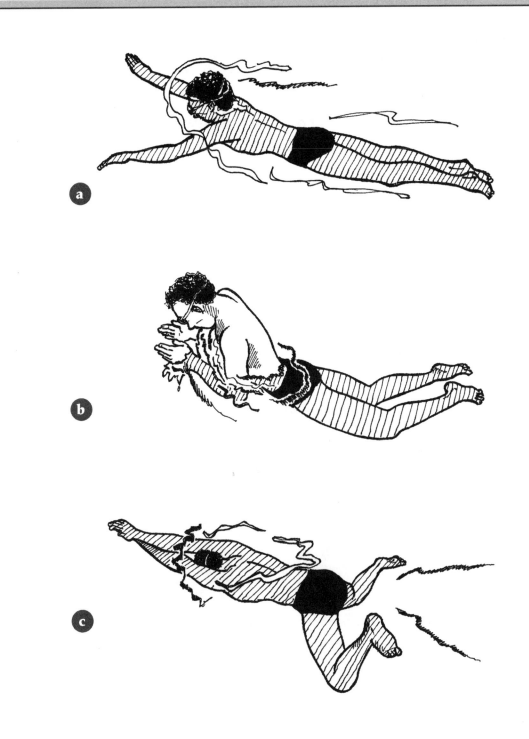

Purpose

To develop the proper timing and extension of the breaststroke. This is a supplemental drill for breaststroke.

Procedure

The kicking action is exactly the same as in drill 72 (Controlled Breaststroke). Now you will add the pulling action to every other kick *(a-f)*.

1. Follow this pattern: pull, breathe, kick, slide and then kick, slide. Hold each slide for a count of three.
2. Keep your nose down, eyes looking down at the bottom. On the slide, the back of your head should be at the surface.

Focus Points

- Kick with an even rhythm.
- Keep your hands in a steady position when not pulling. Locking the thumbs helps.
- Keep the pull quick, and get plenty of lift.
- Control your head position.

Tips

- Keep track of the number of kicks you take each lap. Determine your average. Try to decrease the number each time you practice this drill.
- Use this drill as part of your warm-up before a race. It will help you to feel how you slide through the water after each kick.

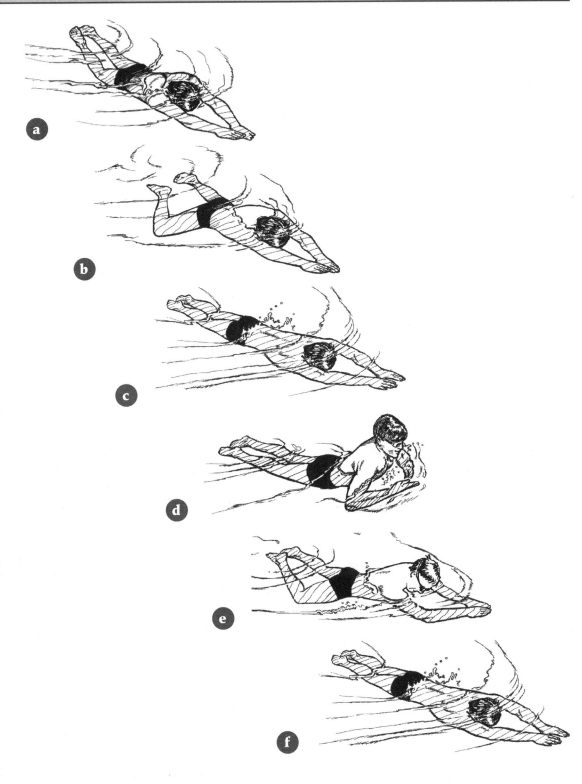

Purpose

To emphasize the hip action needed for the different dolphin breaststrokes by combining the breaststroke and butterfly. Not all swimmers will feel comfortable with this technique, which uses more of a dolphin action with the hips. This is not a key drill, but for many swimmers, depending on their strengths and weaknesses, it may be extremely effective.

Procedure

1. Put on fins. Start off on your front by dolphin kicking in a streamline position (*a*). Take a breaststroke pull, and breathe while you pull (*b*).
2. As you recover, drive your head down into the water, push your hips up, and then finish with the downward part of the dolphin kick. Be sure to stretch your arms out far in front of you (*c*). As you kick down, begin to pull again. Continue to repeat.

Focus Points

- Stretch forward with your arms.
- Get your hips and legs up on every kick.
- Keep the pulling action quick.
- Try to stay up fairly high, and resist going too deep under the surface.

Tips

- To get a better sense of the proper rhythm, try breathing every other pull or every third pull.
- The rhythm of this drill will vary depending on your ease with the dolphin kick. For those who are very comfortable with this action, the rhythm can be quite quick.

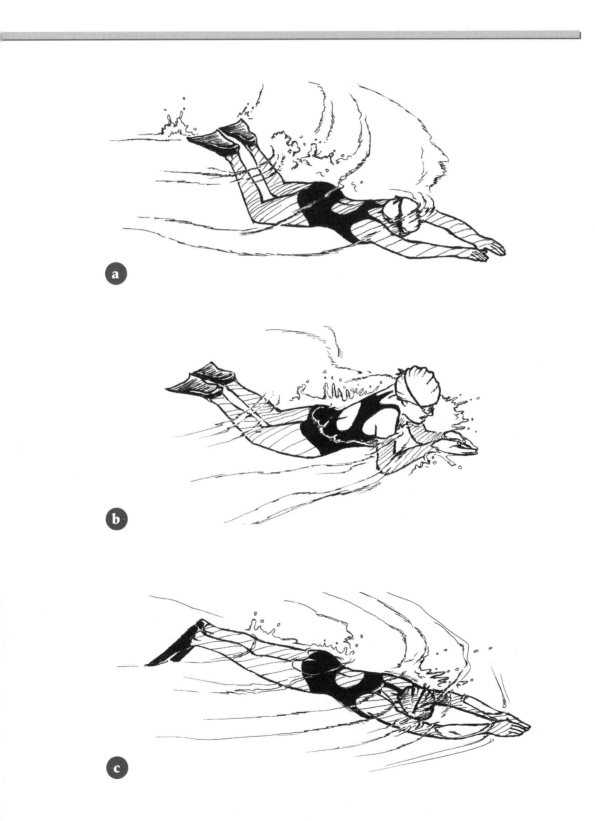

chapter 7

Butterfly

When performed correctly, the butterfly is perhaps the most graceful and beautiful of all the strokes to watch. However, it is also the most difficult stroke for swimmers to master. It requires the most arm strength to lift the body above the surface, and the proper timing can require considerable practice.

The best butterfliers

- have excellent serpentine body action and move through the water with a fluid wave action;
- have strong kicks, generating power from the hips;
- have good head position, looking primarily down and keeping the chin tucked in while breathing; and
- recover their arms with the elbows up and thumbs down.

The following drills will help you achieve all of these fundamentals in your strokes in addition to excellent timing.

Purpose

To feel the body action of the butterfly stroke while at the surface. This is a modification of drill 23 from chapter 2, and it is a key drill in beginning the butterfly series.

Procedure

1. This drill has the same body action as in drill 23 (Dolphin Drill), except you add breathing in sync.
2. Imagine yourself as a dolphin swimming at the surface on the ocean.
3. Put on fins. Take a deep breath. Push off the wall on your front side along the surface, keeping your hands down by your sides and looking down at the bottom of the pool. Just the back of your head will break the surface (a). Do not use your arms on this drill.
4. Use your head to start the body action. Push downward with the forehead to start the whiplike action of the kick (b). Keep the head angle changing, but primarily look down. As you push your forehead down, allow the hips to come up (c). Then, allow your heels to slide above the surface, and begin to kick down (d). Your head will begin to come back up to break the surface as you kick down.
5. Break the surface with your head, and repeat.
6. Your body will "stitch" the surface of the water. Your head, then shoulders, then hips, and then heels will all break the surface in progression with each kick. Keep the motion fluid. You will break the surface in the following pattern: head, shoulders, hips, and heels.
7. Go as far as you can with one breath, breathe, and then repeat.
8. Then work on breathing every third kick with a consistency of rhythm.
9. After you breathe, bring your forehead into the water first—forehead first.

Focus Points

- Be sure to keep your head moving at all times.
- Look down at the black line on the bottom of the pool. If you look forward, your hips cannot create enough power for a strong kick.
- Remember to move with your forehead first.
- Develop a steady rhythm.

Tip

Work on being able to breathe in sync with this drill, once every three kicks. It will help you when you get to the other butterfly drills.

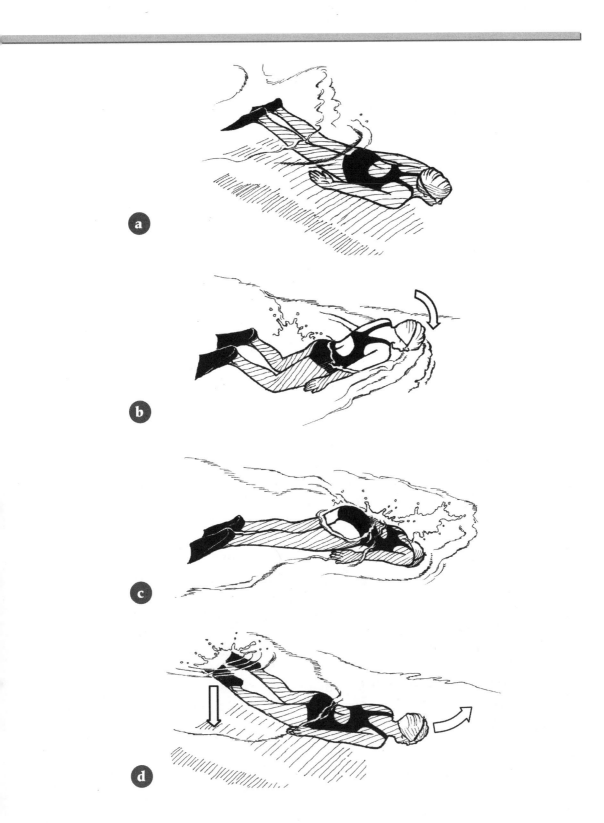

a

b

c

d

Purpose

To develop the feel of the body action of the butterfly while in the extended position and to set up the body position for the pulling action of the stroke.

Procedure

This drill is the same as the previous drill, with one exception: Your arms are extended out in front.

1. Put on fins. Stretch your arms out in front with your hands shoulder-width apart, elbows straight, palms facing down and out at about 45 degrees, and shoulders relaxed.
2. Inhale deeply. As you exhale, push off the wall on your front side along the surface, keeping your hands stretched out in front of you and looking down at the bottom of the pool. Just the back of your head will break the surface (a). Your arms should stay extended throughout the drill with no pulling or sculling action.
3. Use your head to start the body action. Push downward with the forehead to start the whiplike action of the kick (b). Keep the head angle changing, but primarily look down. As you push your forehead down, allow the hips to come up (c). Then allow your heels to slide above the surface, and begin to kick down. Your head will begin to come back up to break the surface as you kick down.
4. Break the surface with your head, and repeat.
5. Your body will "stitch" the surface of the water. Your head, then shoulders, then hips, then heels will all break the surface in progression with each kick. Keep the motion fluid. You will break the surface in the following pattern: head, shoulders, hips, and heels.
6. Go as far as you can with one breath, breathe, then repeat.
7. Then work on breathing every third kick with a consistency of rhythm.
8. After you breathe, bring your forehead into the water first—forehead first.

Focus Points

- Keep your head moving at all times.
- Look down at the black line on the bottom of the pool. If you look forward, your hips cannot create enough power for a strong kick.
- Remember to move with your forehead first.
- Develop a steady rhythm.

Tip

Work on being able to breathe in sync with this drill, once every three kicks, to help you when you get to the other butterfly drills.

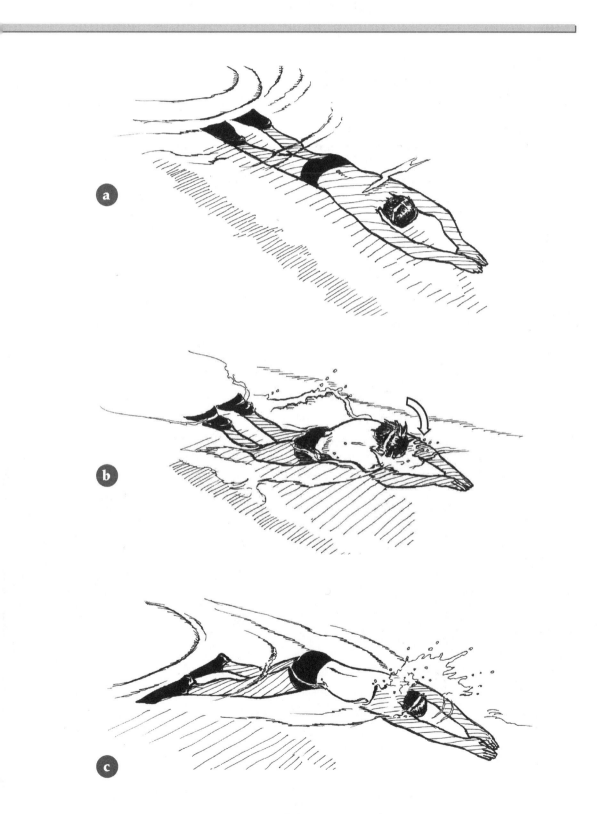

Purpose

To set up a teaching tool that can safely enhance teaching the proper body action of the butterfly.

Procedure

Over the years, I have used all kinds of tools to teach the butterfly action. Following is my simple invention that seems to work very well and helps to correct sunken hips and inverted butterfly strokes.

1. Here's what you'll need to make your own butterfly device:
   - A 9-foot section of quarter-inch nylon rope
   - A pair of pliers
   - Two short bungee cords
   - A hollow, spongy water noodle with a smooth surface
2. Pass the rope through the middle of the noodle so that you have an even amount of rope on either end.
3. Tie a cinch knot on each side of the noodle so that the knot is close to the noodle and keeps the noodle from sliding in either direction.
4. Tie a loop knot on each end of the rope.
5. Attach one end of a bungee cord on each loop, and clamp down using some pliers. Now the butterfly device is ready for attachment!
6. Place the device perpendicularly across a lane by hooking the bungee cords on the cable of the lane rope. I usually place the device about 6 yards away from the wall.

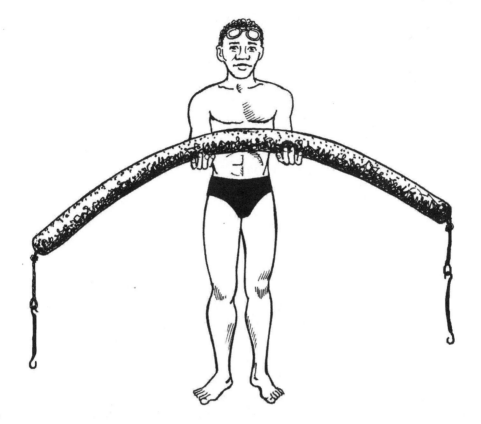

Purpose
To develop the sine-wave body action of the butterfly with the lift of the arm pull. This drill also helps to correct the inverted butterfly action that makes you drop your hips.

Procedure
This drill was inspired by watching the salmon run on the American River. It was amazing to watch these fish—some of them 30 to 40 pounds—hurl their bodies through the air as they leapt over the waterfalls and up the river. What power! What if swimmers could generate that much power and lift while swimming the butterfly? Thus this drill was invented. It is basically an aquatic high jump!

1. Position the butterfly device across the lane about 6 yards away from the wall. It's also helpful to place some sort of marker (such as a diving brick) directly under the device on the bottom.
2. Put on fins. Start at the wall facing into the lane.
3. Push off underwater on your front as in drill 76 (Superman Fly)—about 2 or 3 feet deep. Start your dolphin kicking action (*a*).
4. When you get close to the butterfly device, start to angle yourself upward so that your hands are headed right for the device and your head will break the surface just in front of the device (*b, c*).
5. Just as your hands almost touch the device, pull your arms down as hard as you can, all the way to your thighs. Create as much power as you can to lift your body over the noodle as cleanly as possible—preferably not even touching it! Go over the noodle headfirst, then curl your forehead down so that your forehead enters the water first (forehead first). Follow with the hips and finally the legs (*d, e*).
6. Once your body clears the noodle, kick downward with a dolphin kick (*f*).
7. Kick a couple more dolphin kicks while underwater, then stop.

Focus Points
- Be sure to start off deep enough underwater so you can create the power from your pull.
- Breathe very quickly.
- Remember to enter forehead first after you clear the noodle.
- Relax the legs as you clear the noodle, then kick after you clear it.

Tip
Practice this drill until you can go over the noodle smoothly and easily.

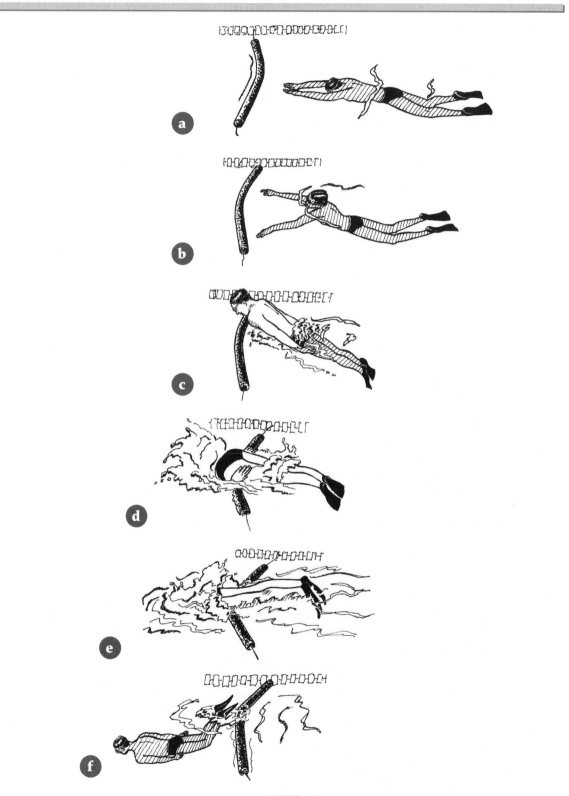

Purpose

To develop the power from the arm pull along with the timing of the body action of the butterfly.

Procedure

This drill is the same as drill 78 (Salmon Fly With Device), except you don't use the device and you repeat the action down the lane.

1. Put on fins. Start at the wall facing into the lane.
2. Push off underwater on your front in the Superman Fly position—about 2 to 3 feet deep. Start your dolphin kicking action.
3. Do about three or four dolphin kicks underwater and then start to approach the surface. When you get close to the surface (imagine the butterfly device being there), start to angle yourself upward so that your hands are headed for the surface.
4. Just as your hands almost touch the surface, pull your arms down as hard as you can, all the way to your thighs. Create as much power as you can so that you can lift your body over the imaginary noodle as cleanly as possible (*a*). Break the surface headfirst, then curl your forehead down so that your forehead enters the water first (forehead first) (*b*). Follow with the hips and finally the legs (*c*).
5. Once your body clears the surface, kick downward with a dolphin kick.
6. Kick a couple more dolphin kicks while underwater and then extend your arms in front again.
7. Repeat the sequence down the lane.

Focus Points

- Start deep enough underwater so that you can create the power from your pull.
- Breathe very quickly.
- Enter forehead first after you break the surface.
- Relax the legs as you break the surface, then kick after your hips reenter the water.

Tip

Be very relaxed underwater, then explode through the surface with great power from your pull.

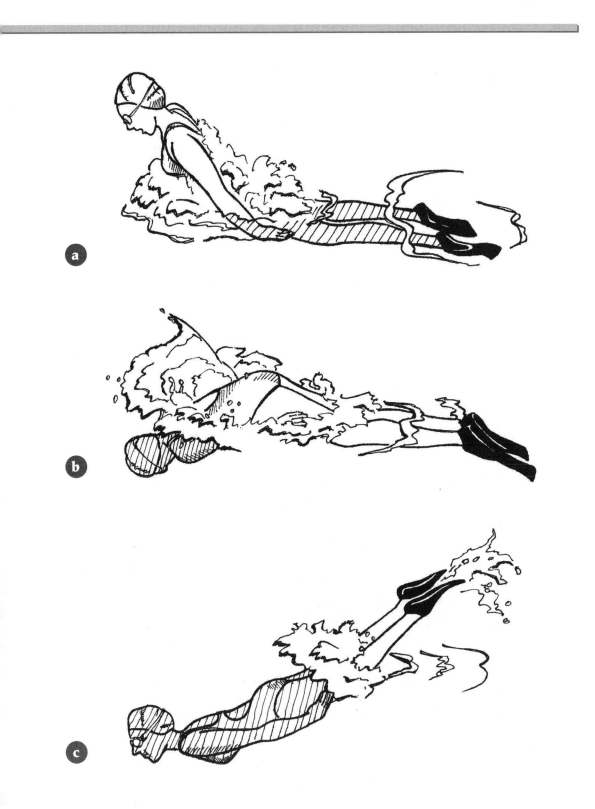

Purpose

To teach proper mechanics of the arm stroke, particularly the recovery and entry.

Procedure

The most common butterfly arm stroke fault is the hugging recovery. It occurs when the arms recover with the thumbs turned upward and the palms facing forward—just like giving a hug. Recovering this way makes the stroke less effective. This drill works to eliminate that type of entry.

1. Lean forward a little, bending at the waist. Place your hands on your knees. Raise your arms so that the backs of the hands (knuckle side) are turned inward (a).
2. Simultaneously sweep both arms outward to about twice shoulder-width apart. Bend the elbows a little and rotate the hands inward to press back toward the waist (b). Continue to sweep the hands back, passing by the hips.
3. The arms will continue to press back until they are straight back and the palms are facing up (c). At this point, the hands should be as close together as possible.
4. The recovery phase begins by first relaxing the wrists and turning the arms so that the wrists lead the motion and the thumbs are pointing downward and back.
5. Keeping the elbows straight and the arms level, move the arms forward until they are directly in front of each shoulder (d). This completes the cycle.

Focus Points

- Maintain strength in the wrists during the pulling phase, and keep them straight.
- Finish the pull with the palms facing up.
- Relax the wrists on the recovery.
- Let the wrists lead the recovery; the thumbs are pointing downward and back.

Tips

- Practice this drill slowly.
- Try practicing this drill in the water while standing up with your shoulders just above the surface.

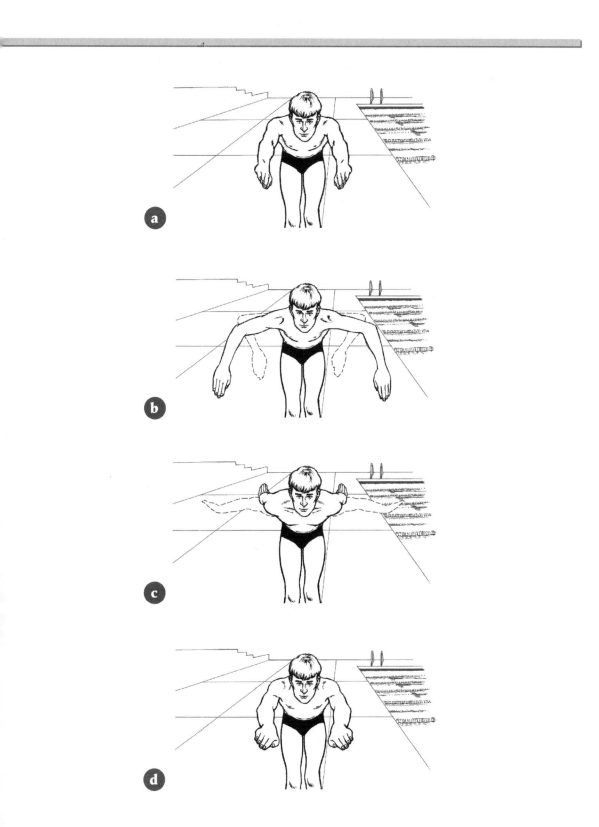

Purpose

To develop the proper body action for the butterfly stroke combined with the arm pull.

Procedure

This drill has the same set up as drill 78 (Salmon Fly With Device), except that you add the complete arm stroke.

1. Position the butterfly device across the lane about 6 yards away from the wall. It is also helpful to place some sort of marker (e.g., a diving brick) directly under the device on the bottom.
2. Put on fins. Start at the wall facing into the lane.
3. Push off underwater on your front in the Superman Fly position—about 2 or 3 feet deep (a). Start your dolphin kicking action.
4. When you get close to the butterfly device, start to angle yourself upward so that your hands are headed straight for the device and your head will break the surface just in front of the device (b).
5. Just as your hands almost touch the device, pull your arms through a complete stroke and recover over the noodle (c, d). Create as much power as you can so that you can lift your body over the noodle as cleanly as possible—preferably not even touching it! Go over the noodle headfirst, then curl your forehead down so that your forehead enters the water first (forehead first) at about the same time that your arms reenter the water (e). Follow with the hips and finally the legs (f).
6. Once your body clears the noodle, kick downward with a dolphin kick.
7. Kick a couple more dolphin kicks while underwater, then stop.

Focus Points

- Start off deep enough underwater so that you can create the power from your pull.
- Breathe very quickly.
- Enter forehead first after you clear the noodle.
- Relax the legs as you clear the noodle, then kick after you clear it.

Tip

Practice this drill until you can go over the noodle smoothly and easily.

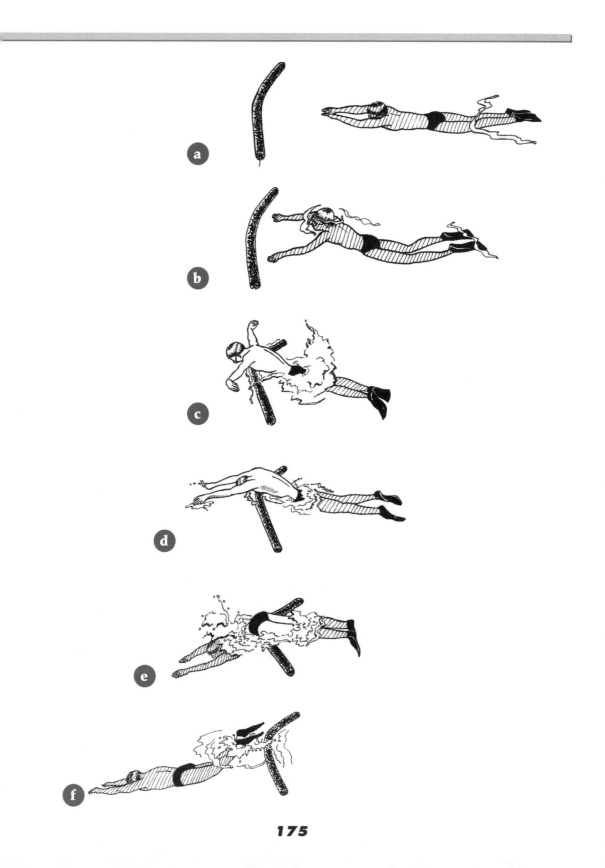

Purpose

To add the arm pull and recovery to the butterfly body action.

Procedure

This drill has the same action as the previous drill, but you use no device and you continue repeating the pull and recovery down the length of the pool.

1. Put on fins. Start at the wall facing into the lane.
2. Push off underwater on your front in the Superman Fly position—about 2 or 3 feet deep (a). Start your dolphin kicking action. Do three or four dolphin kicks underwater, then move toward the surface to breathe.
3. Just as you reach the surface with your hands, pull with both arms to lift your body (b). Breathe when you reach the peak of your lift (c). As you finish the pull and begin the butterfly recovery with the arms, return your head down into the water, entering forehead first.
4. By the time you reach the dive, your arms are in front of you again and your head is down. Lock the thumbs up again right away. Get the hips up (d).
5. Finish the stroke with a strong kick. Look down while kicking under the water.
6. Repeat with three or four dolphin kicks underwater. Then, come to the surface and repeat the sequence. The sequence will now be pull, breathe, dive, kick.

Focus Points

- Remember this sequence: pull, breathe, dive, kick.
- Look down while kicking under the water.
- Get your forehead into the water first after breathing.
- After breathing, get your hips up above the surface.

Tip

- Perform this drill by going across the width of the pool over alternate loose lane ropes. Begin to pull just as you reach the lane rope. Do not touch the rope with your arms; swim over it. This drill is fun and gives you good practice. Try to touch the lane rope as little as possible.

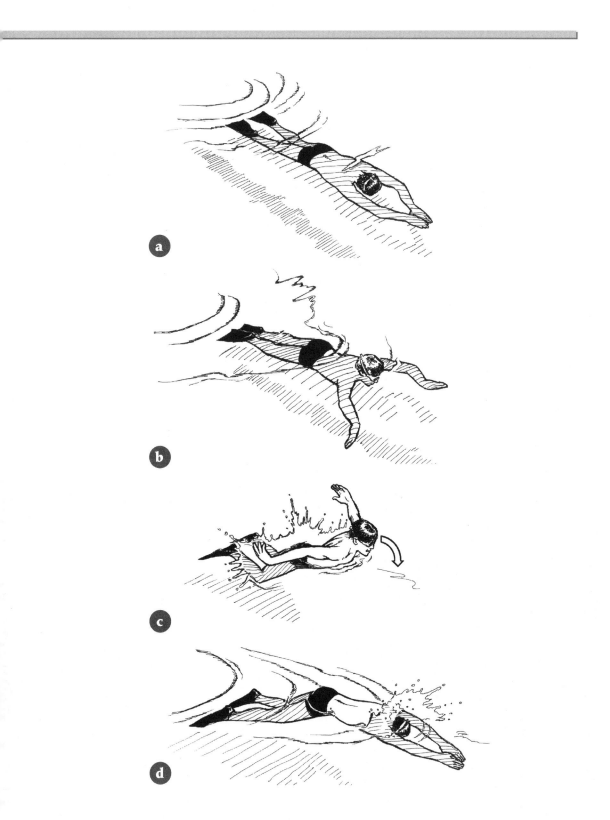

Purpose

To transition to the continuous body action of the butterfly at the surface while gradually incorporating the arm action.

Procedure

1. Put on fins. Keep one arm out in front of you at all times, while using the other arm to pull (*a*).
2. Stay on the surface, and keep the rhythm of pull, breathe, dive, kick in a continuous fashion.
3. Breathe to the side of the pulling arm (*b, c*). Briefly lock the thumbs each time you dive until you feel the kick.
4. Relax, and go slowly. Look down when you dive. Lift the hips up after breathing (*d*).
5. Repeat the cycle for the other arm.

Focus Points

- Maintain the rhythm: pull, breathe, dive, kick.
- Look down after you breathe.
- Lift your hips up after breathing.
- Lock your thumbs each time until you feel the kick.

Tip

Alternate arms every lap, then every four strokes.

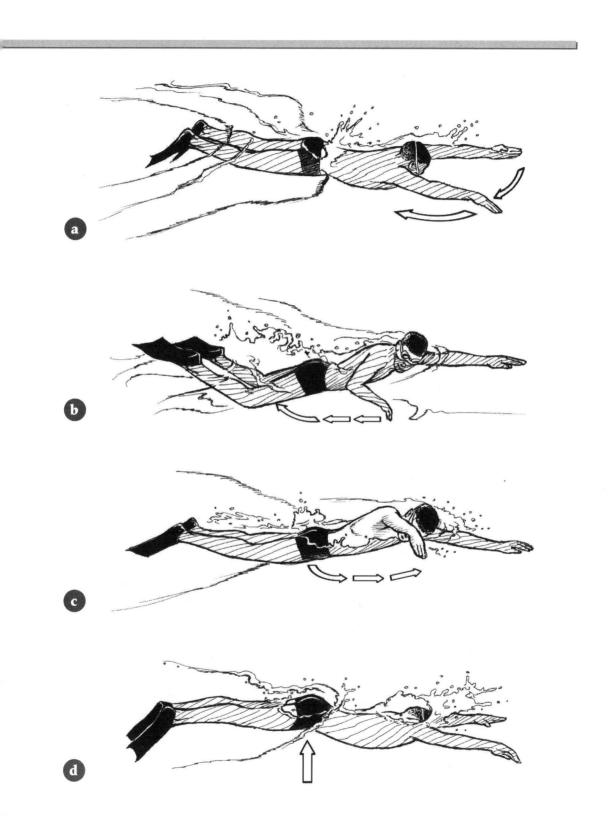

Purpose

To continue the transition to a complete butterfly by focusing on the body action.

Procedure

This drill combines the action of drill 83 (One-Arm Butterfly) with the two-arm recovery.

1. Put your fins on.
2. Stay on the surface and concentrate on maintaining the rhythm of pull, breathe, dive, kick in a continuous fashion.
3. First, take two strokes (pull and recovery) with one arm *(a)*, then two strokes with the other arm *(b)*, and finally two strokes with both arms *(c)*. Continue to repeat this cycle.
4. Try to breathe every other stroke. Breathe straight ahead when taking the two-arm stroke; breathe to the side when taking the one-arm stroke. Lock the thumbs up on each stroke when you dive until you feel the kick.
5. Relax, and go slowly. Lift the hips up on each stroke as your hands come together in front.

Focus Points

- Concentrate on the rhythm: pull, breathe, dive, kick.
- Look down and lift your hips up as your hands come together.
- Lock your thumbs each time until you feel the kick.

Tip

See how slowly you can do this drill with control. Try to be very smooth.

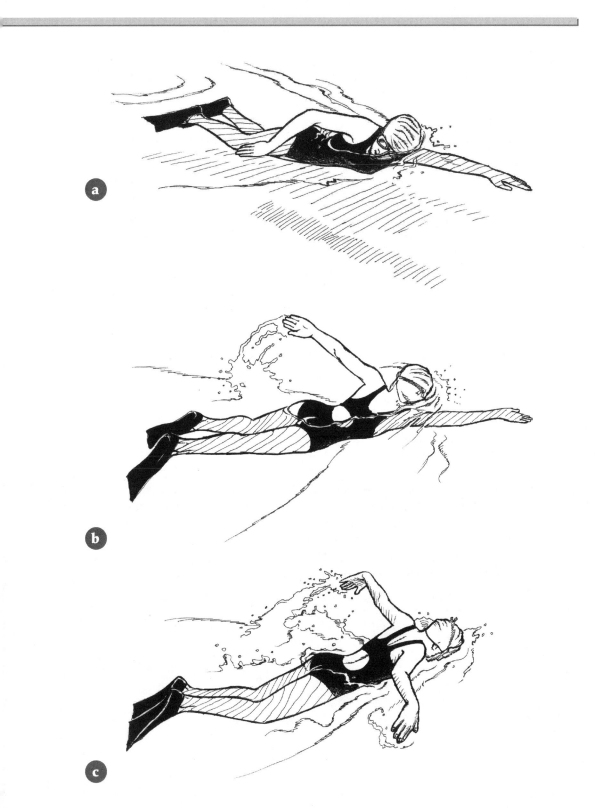

Purpose

To complete the transition to a controlled butterfly with excellent rhythm. The emphasis remains on the body action.

Procedure

This drill simply eliminates the one-arm action of the previous drill.

1. Put your fins on. Use both arms for every stroke. Stay on the surface and work on keeping the rhythm of pull, breathe, dive, kick in a continuous fashion (a, b).
2. Try to breathe every other stroke. Lock your thumbs up briefly on each stroke when you dive. Relax, and go slowly. Lift your hips up on each stroke as your hands come together.
3. As you become stronger, try using this rhythm: reach, kick. As your arms enter the water, that is the reach. As the feet kick down, that is the kick (c). The timing between the reach and kick should be very even.

Focus Points

- Keep a nice, flowing rhythm: pull, breathe, dive, kick.
- Eventually use this rhythm: reach, kick.
- Look down after each breath.
- Lift your hips up on each stroke.
- Lock your thumbs on each stroke until you feel the kick.

Tip

Stay relaxed. Let the stroke technique do the work for you. You may notice that as you swim a little faster, a second kick in the middle of each stroke will usually occur naturally. However, in doing this drill, you don't need to focus on the second kick. For most, this second kick is a minor kick that gives balance to the rhythm of the stroke. For some, the second kick can become very strong. It is usually best to first focus on a nice, fluid motion.

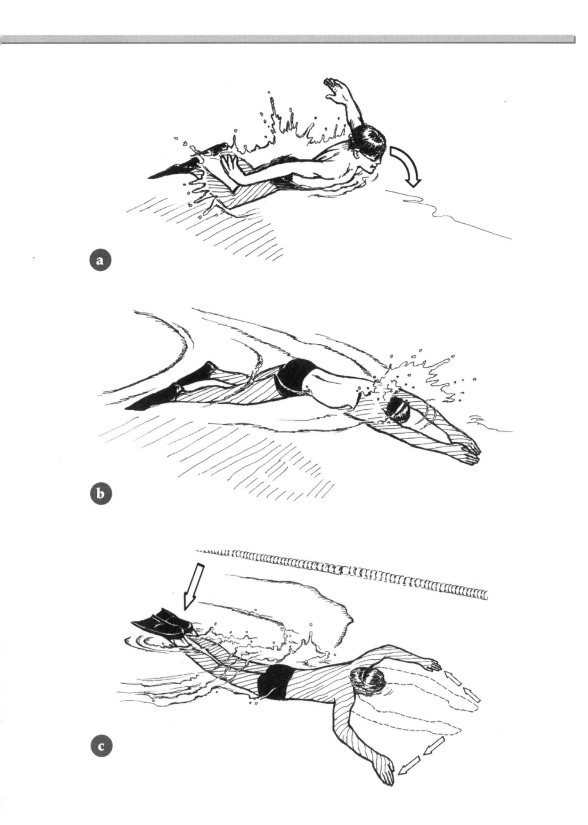

chapter 8

Freestyle and Backstroke Turns

Approximately one-quarter of a race involves starts, turns, and finishes. These maneuvers require skill, precision, and speed. Even small errors in execution can easily separate the champion from the average swimmer. Swimmers must consistently practice good starts, turns, and finishes.

These drills teach you how to

- perform a proper flip (somersault) for both the freestyle and backstroke turns,
- control your breathing while approaching the wall on the freestyle turn,
- approach the wall smoothly and accurately for the backstroke turn, and
- land your feet properly at the wall and push off to a streamline position.

This chapter will address the most frequently performed turn—the freestyle turn—as well as the most troublesome turn—the backstroke turn. The following drills provide a systematic approach to mastering the fundamentals of these turns.

Purpose

To develop the quickness needed to get into a proper streamline position in preparation for the streamline push-offs from the wall.

Procedure

1. Stand in shallow water so that you are at least waist deep but not more than shoulder depth.
2. Lift your arms so that your hands are at your sides near your shoulders, and bend your knees in preparation for a jump (a).
3. Jump straight up. As you jump, extend your arms upward into a streamline position (b). You should reach the streamline by the time you reach the peak of your jump. Hold the streamline as you land (c), then release.
4. Repeat at least 10 times.

Focus Points

- Jump straight up and as high as you can.
- Work on getting into a perfect streamline as quickly as possible.

Tips

- Do this drill facing a partner, and have a third person or a coach tell you when to jump. Challenge each other to get into the streamline more quickly.
- Stand underneath the backstroke flags if the depth works for you. When you jump, see whether you are going straight up and touching the flags each time.

Purpose

To develop speed in performing the somersault and to get a sense of how to somersault more quickly through the air.

Procedure

This drill is advanced. You should be able to do a basic somersault before attempting this drill. And, it's lots of fun!

1. Stand in shallow water so that you are at least waist deep but not more than shoulder depth.
2. Bend your knees in preparation for a jump *(a)*.
3. Jump straight up. As you jump, drive your head down between your knees as you perform a complete somersault *(b-e)*. Try to do the somersault as high out of the water as possible. Land on your feet.
4. Repeat at least 10 times. Be sure to pause a little in between jumps so you don't get too dizzy!

Focus Points

- Your body will travel faster through the air than it will through the water. Work on having your body somersault through the air as much as possible.
- The faster your body flips over, the better. Speed!

Tip

Do this drill facing a partner. Have plenty of space between you. Have a third person or a coach tell you when to jump. Challenge each other to get faster.

Purpose

To develop the control of the body position going into the turn and to use the head and abdominals in performing the flip.

Procedure

Before beginning this drill, it is often helpful to review drill 6 (Sliding).

1. Start at the wall with one hand on the wall, ready to push off.
2. Push off the wall, at the surface, on your front, with your nose down and arms down at your sides (*a*). Travel along the surface for 4 to 5 yards.
3. Using your head to start the action, drive the head down and under you to perform a complete somersault (*b-e*).
4. Come to a stop, and breathe.
5. Return to the wall, and repeat as necessary.

Focus Points

- Absolutely do not lift your head to breathe until after you complete the somersault.
- Drive your head down quickly to start the somersault. Your somersault should be in a fairly tight tuck position. Do the somersault as high as possible with your body traveling mostly through the air rather than the water.

Tip

As you perform the somersault, exhale and squeeze the abdominals.

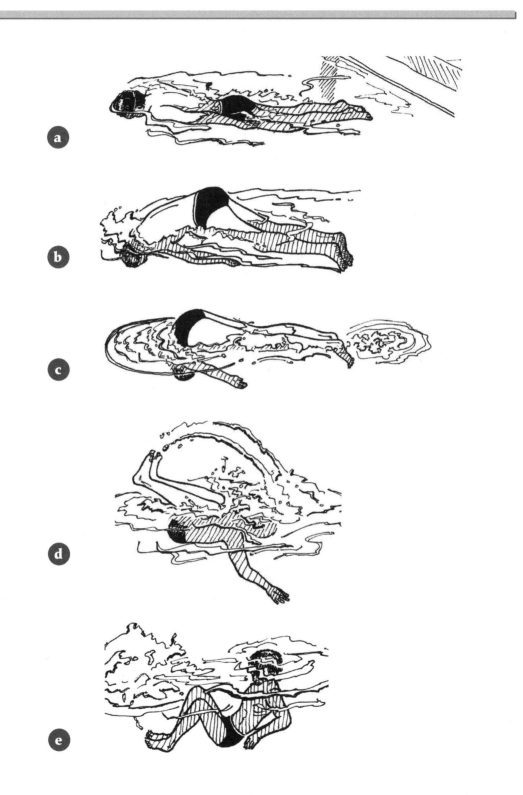

Purpose

To develop the next step in the sequence: performing the flip starting from an extended position.

Procedure

This drill is the same as the previous drill, except you extend one arm.

1. Start at the wall with one hand on the wall, ready to push off.
2. Push off the wall, at the surface, on your front, with your nose down and one arm extended forward, the other arm down at your side (*a*). Travel along the surface for 4 to 5 yards.
3. Using your arm to start the action, drive the arm and head down and under you to perform a complete somersault (*b-e*).
4. Come to a stop, and breathe.
5. Return to the wall and repeat as necessary. Switch arms.

Focus Points

- Absolutely do not lift your head to breathe until after you complete the somersault.
- Drive your arm and head down quickly to start the somersault.
- Drive the arm and head at the same time. Avoid the common pitfall of pulling the arm first and then driving the head.
- Keep plenty of lift and speed!

Tip

As you perform the somersault, exhale and squeeze the abdominals.

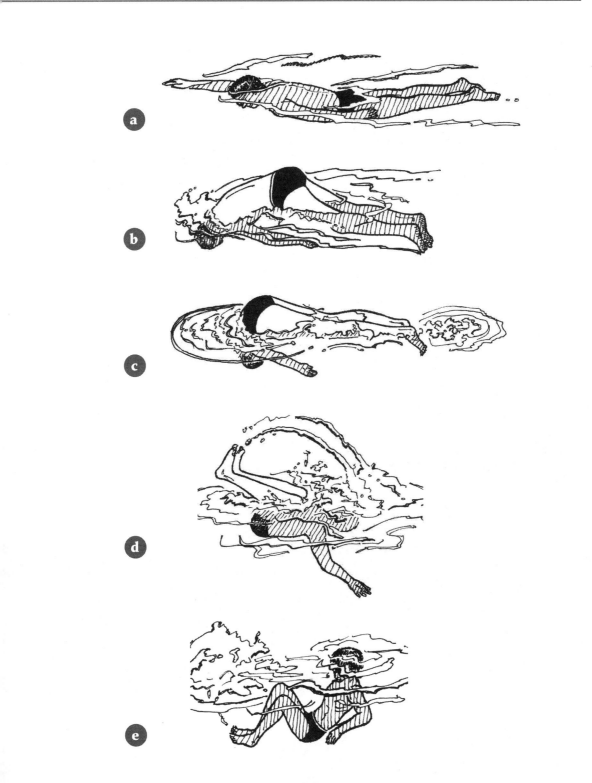

Purpose

To develop the next step in the sequence: to add the flutter kick.

Procedure

This drill is the same as the previous drill, except you add the flutter kick.

1. Start at the wall with one hand on the wall, ready to push off.
2. Push off the wall, at the surface, on your front, with your nose down and one arm extended forward, the other arm down at your side. Kick along the surface for 5 to 6 yards *(a)*.
3. Using your arm to start the action, drive the arm and head down and under you to perform a complete somersault *(b-e)*.
4. Come to a stop, and breathe.
5. Repeat, going back toward the wall. Switch arms.

Focus Points

- Absolutely do not lift your head to breathe until after you complete the somersault.
- Drive your arm and head down quickly to start the somersault.
- Drive the arm and head at the same time. Avoid the common pitfall of pulling the arm first and then driving the head. Keep kicking all the way into the somersault.
- Keep plenty of lift and speed!

Tip

As you perform the somersault, exhale and squeeze the abdominals.

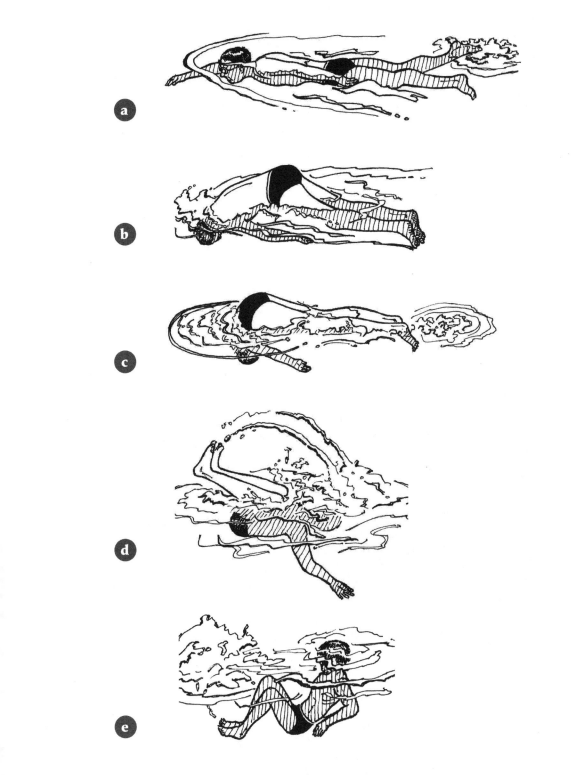

Purpose

To develop the next step in the sequence: to add freestyle swimming before the flip.

Procedure

This drill is the same as the previous drill, except you add three freestyle strokes and a three-count hold. The three-count hold, with kicking, is very important to set up a stretched position before the turn. When the body is stretched, it is higher and therefore able to flip more through the air, which converts to more speed!

1. Start at the wall with one hand on the wall, ready to push off.
2. Push off the wall, at the surface, on your front, with your nose down. Swim three strokes of freestyle, counting each time your hand enters the water as one (a). Then hold the extended position and kick along the surface for a count of three (b).
3. Using your arm to start the action, drive the arm and head down and under you to perform a complete somersault (c-f).
4. Come to a stop, and breathe.
5. Repeat, going back toward the wall. Switch arms.

Focus Points

- Absolutely do not lift your head to breathe until after you complete the somersault.
- Be completely stretched out on the surface after your three strokes.
- Drive your arm and head down quickly to start the somersault.
- Drive the arm and head at the same time. Avoid the common pitfall of pulling the arm first and then driving the head. Keep kicking all the way into the somersault.
- Keep plenty of lift and speed!

Tip

As you perform the somersault, exhale and squeeze the abdominals.

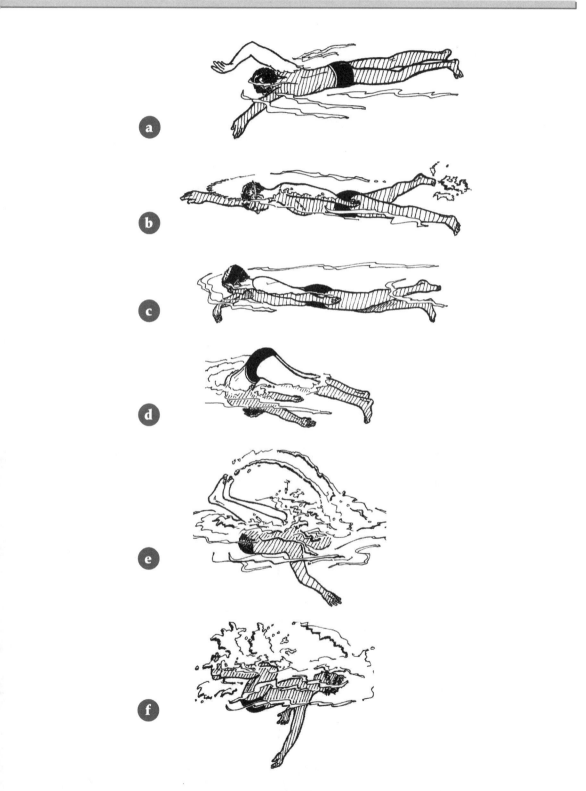

Purpose

This is the next step for the flip turns and will teach the proper method of beginning the backstroke after a start or after a turn.

Procedure

1. Start by pushing off the wall underwater in a streamline position on your back, about 2 feet deep *(a-c)*. As you clear the wall, begin a flutter kick *(d)*.
2. Kick for a count of at least eight, then pull one arm down to your side to begin the backstroke arm action *(e)*.
3. Control your depth so that you break the surface just as you finish your first arm pull *(f)*.
4. Complete about three strokes.
5. Repeat.

Focus Points

- Control your depth.
- Hold a tight streamline for a count of eight or more while kicking.
- Pull only one arm down first before starting your backstroke.

Tip

Once you master this drill with the flutter kick, you can add dolphin kicking in the streamline position and try to get a lot more distance and speed (depending on the individual). However, be sure to control your depth. The dolphin kick is used mostly with the butterfly and the backstroke start, but it is also effective for some swimmers in the freestyle push-off.

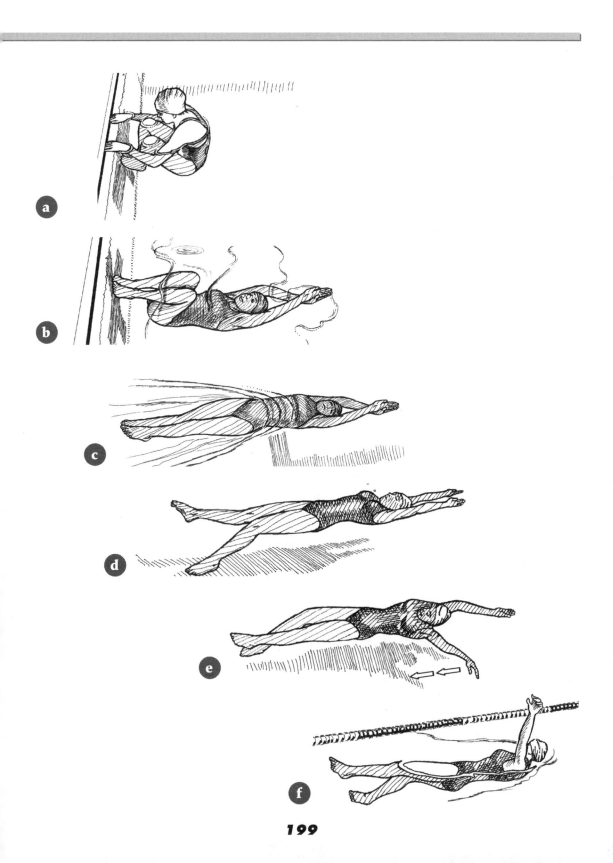

Purpose

This is the next step for developing the flip turn. This drill will reinforce the breathing control on the approach and teach the accurate landing of the feet at the wall.

Procedure

1. Begin about 10 to 12 yards away from the wall. Swim freestyle toward the wall *(a)*. Control your breathing from the flags (5 yards) on in.

2. When you are at least two strokes away from the wall, perform your somersault, having your feet land on the wall about 1 foot below the surface *(b)*. If you are too far away, continue to repeat the approach and gradually turn closer to the wall until you find the right distance for your turn.

3. Do not push off; just land your feet. You should be able to look at your feet while underwater to see where they land on the wall.

4. When your feet land properly on the wall, your body will be in a lounge chair position underwater (on your back with the hips and knees slightly bent), and your hands will be just above your head. Your feet will land about 1 to 2 feet deep, depending on your size *(c)*. (If you are smaller, your feet will be higher; if you are bigger, your feet will be lower.)

Focus Points

- Control your breathing so that you can focus on the wall.
- Perform a quick, high flip.
- Look to see where your feet land.

Tip

Master the ability to pull through the turn with either arm.

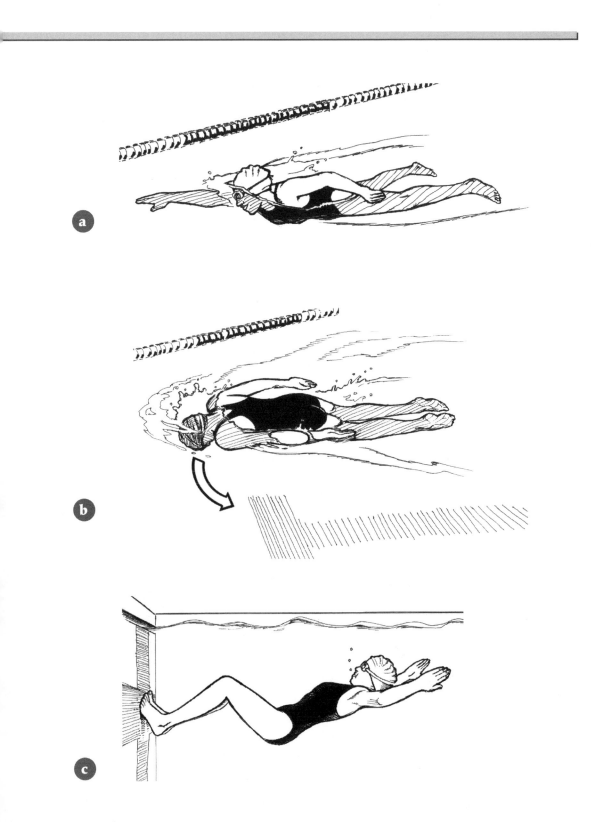

Purpose

This next step for the flip turns is an important drill that should be practiced frequently. It allows you to focus on the proper mechanics of the turn and work on achieving the greatest speed possible.

Procedure

Now you will combine the approach, the foot touch, and the backstroke breakout. It will become a freestyle-to-backstroke turn. This drill is very important because it will help you learn to control your approach, push-off, and eventually speed. Practice doing it correctly several times before you try to increase your speed.

1. Swim freestyle to the wall with the proper breath control (*a*).
2. Perform your flip and land your feet on the wall, just as in the Foot Touch Drill (*b*).
3. Push off underwater into the streamline position (*c*), and start your backstroke breakout (*d*).

Focus Points

- Be in control.
- Look to see where you land before you push off.
- Don't rush it. Practice being accurate first.

Tip

Once you master the mechanics of this drill and consistently place your landing correctly, try to anticipate the wall and begin to push off just before your feet land. This way you will punch off the wall very quickly, which will help you develop the fastest turn possible.

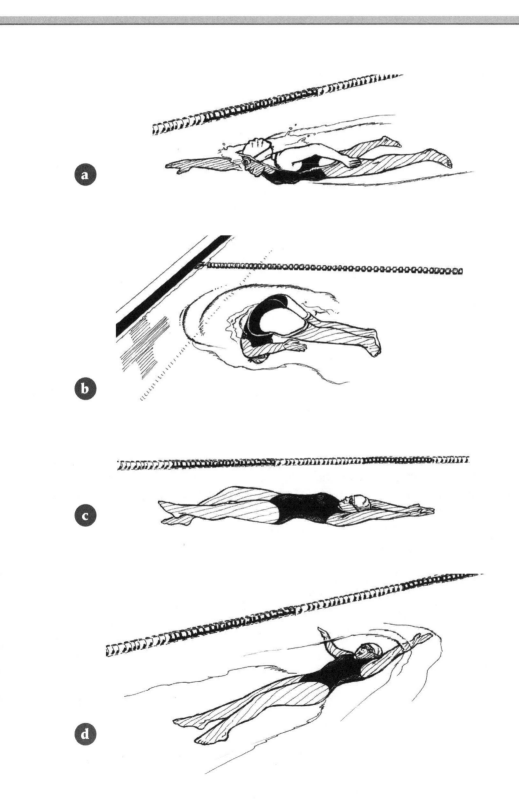

Purpose

This drill is the next step for the freestyle flip turn and will teach an effective method for getting off the wall with the fastest mechanics possible.

Procedure

1. Start by pushing off the wall underwater in a streamline position on your back, about 2 feet deep. As you clear the wall, begin a flutter kick *(a-c)*.
2. Kick for a count of four while holding the streamline position on your back. Then, still holding the streamline, begin to slowly corkscrew (a one-quarter twist) to your side while counting another four *(d-f)*. Then, start to come to the surface and pull the lower arm down in a freestyle stroke as your body rotates to your front.
3. Control your depth so that you break the surface just as you finish your first arm pull.
4. Complete about three strokes of freestyle.
5. Repeat.

Focus Points

- Control your depth.
- Hold a tight streamline for a count of four on your back and for another count of four as you corkscrew while kicking.

Tip

Once you master this drill with the flutter kick, you can add dolphin kicking in the streamline position and try to get a lot more distance and speed (depending on the individual). However, be sure to control your depth. The dolphin kick is used mostly with the butterfly and the backstroke start but is also effective for some swimmers in the freestyle push-off. You may want to use a combination of a few dolphin kicks followed by flutter kicking. It depends on the individual.

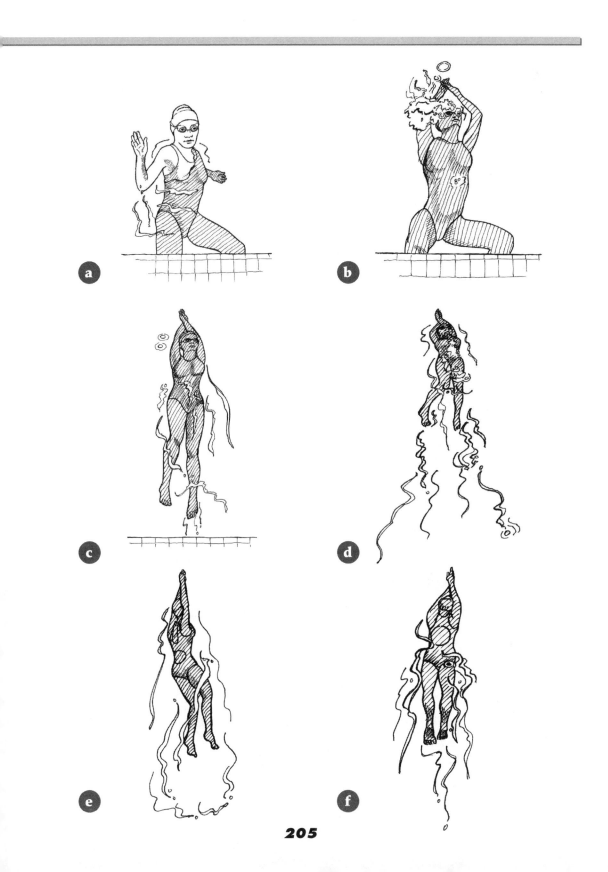

Purpose
To complete the process for the freestyle turn.

Procedure
It is important to realize that the rules do not require you to be on your front when you leave the wall. Because twisting on the wall slows the turn, this drill will focus on rotating the body after the push-off from the wall, during the streamline portion of the turn. Review drill 94 (Freestyle-to-Backstroke Turn).

1. Start out about 10 to 12 yards away from the wall.
2. Swim freestyle to the wall with proper breath control *(a)*.
3. Perform your flip, and land your feet on the wall *(b, c)*.
4. Push off underwater into a streamline position on your back *(d, e)*.
5. Kick for a count of four while holding the streamline position on your back. Then, still holding the streamline, begin to slowly corkscrew (a one-quarter twist) to your side while counting another four *(f)*. Then, start to come to the surface and pull the lower arm down in a freestyle stroke as your body rotates to your front *(g)*.
6. Control your depth so that you break the surface just as you finish your first arm pull.
7. Complete about three strokes of freestyle.

Focus Points
- Push off while still on your back.
- Rotate your body after you clear the wall, not while on the wall.

Tips
- Focus on the mechanics first before trying to increase your speed.
- Try to control your breathing for the first two or three strokes after your turn as well.

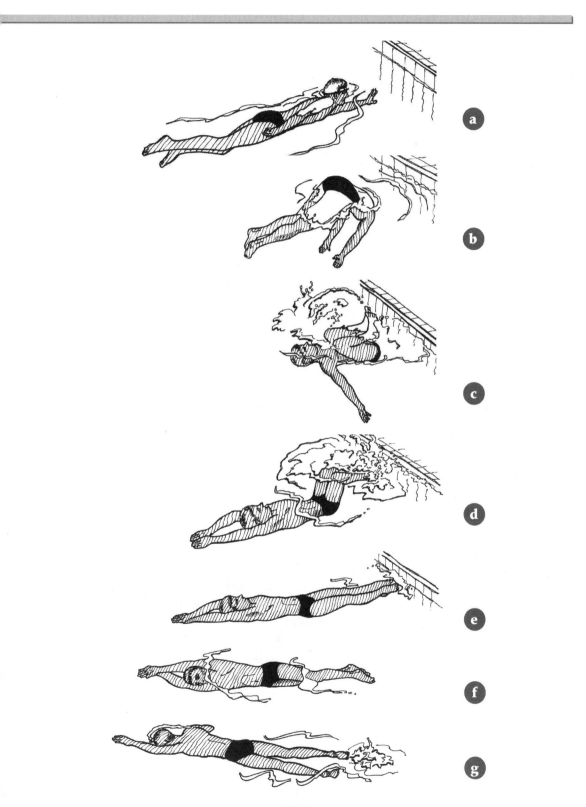

Purpose

To teach you a safe method to determine the stroke count from the flags to the wall for the backstroke finish. This stroke count is important for both the finish and the turn.

Procedure

1. Start at the middle of the pool. Swim backstroke at full speed toward the wall.

2. Just as you pass directly underneath the backstroke flags, begin to count your strokes. At first, take just two strokes past the flags and then kick in the rest of the way, with your arm extended *(a)*.

3. Finish by letting your hand touch the wall with your fingers pointing down. Bend the elbow of the up arm just a little as you kick in on your last stroke *(b)*. You should not have to look back for the wall at all. Just focus on the flags and your stroke count.

4. If you have plenty of room, add one more stroke the next time. As long as you have a safe amount of room remaining, continue to add one stroke at a time until you reach a safe number of strokes.

5. Be consistent in how you count the number of strokes you take from the flags. Ideally, on your last stroke, your hand will enter the water between 1 and 3 feet away from the wall. This will be a safe finish.

Focus Points

- Practice this drill at full speed.
- Kick in hard.
- Focus on the flags, not the wall.
- Be consistent in how you count your strokes.
- Know your stroke count!

Tip

It is better to take fewer, more powerful strokes with lots of strong kicking than a greater number of choppy, short strokes. Try to establish the lowest number of strokes with great speed and complete safety.

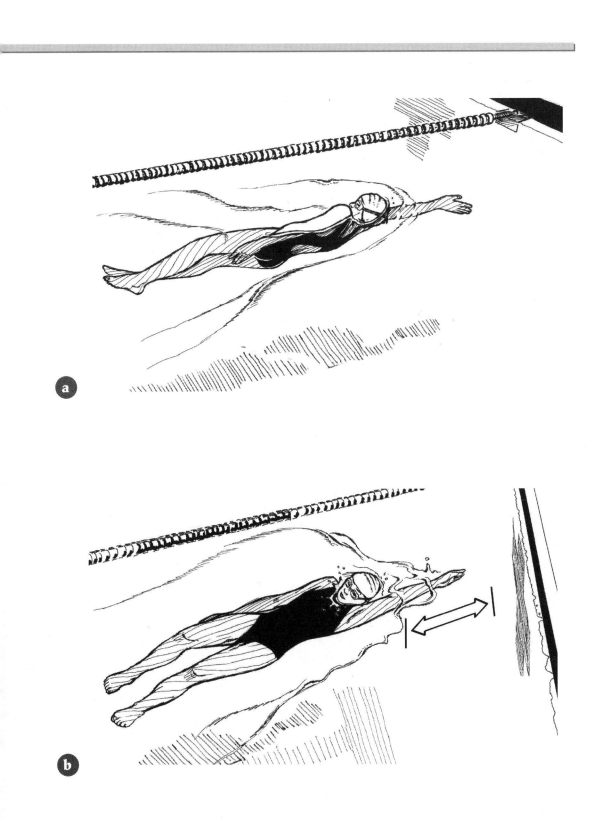

Purpose

To practice rolling properly onto the stomach before performing the backstroke flip turn.

This is called corkscrew swimming, because you twist and spiral through the water just as a corkscrew twists through a cork.

Procedure

1. Start by swimming one arm stroke of freestyle on your front (a).
2. While flutter kicking, turn your head to breathe, and keep turning your head and body so that you are on your back (b, c).
3. Recover the down arm using a backstroke recovery, and pull with the up arm.
4. Continue to turn your head and body in the same direction until you are completely on your front side. This completes one corkscrew stroke.
5. Taking very smooth and controlled strokes, swim the corkscrew stroke in one direction for four strokes, and then swim the corkscrew stroke in the other direction. Repeat this several times.

Focus Points

- Keep the stroke smooth.
- Keep a steady kick.

Tip

See how few corkscrew strokes you can take per lap. The fewer, the better.

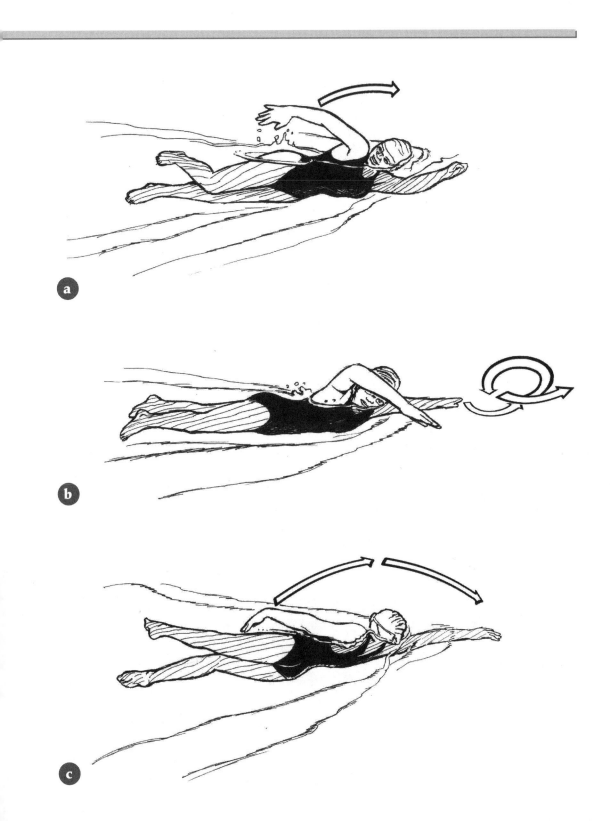

Purpose

To complete the process for the backstroke turn.

Procedure

Now you will be able to complete the backstroke turn. Remember what your stroke count is for the backstroke finish. It should be the same total number of strokes that you will take for the turn. However, you might need to make a minor adjustment to the number of strokes you take for the turn.

1. Subtract one from your stroke count for the backstroke finish. This number will be the number of backstroke arm strokes you will take from the flags while still on your back.

2. After your arm enters the water for the last arm stroke, you roll to that same side. Then, with the other arm, take one corkscrew stroke (freestyle recovery) to get to your stomach (a, b).

3. Now you are in position to do your flip, just as in drill 94 (Freestyle-to-Backstroke Turn) (c-e). The total number of strokes for your turn should be the same as for your finish.

4. Practice this drill first in the open water before trying it at the wall. Keep the strokes smooth.

5. If you find that you are consistently too far away from the wall, you may need to add a stroke. If you find that you are consistently too close, you should subtract a stroke. Once you push off, complete the backstroke breakout.

Focus Points

- Keep a steady stroke rhythm.
- Keep a strong kick.
- Focus on consistency.

Tip

Roll very smoothly and gradually. Remember that the action must be continuous once your shoulders are past the vertical position.

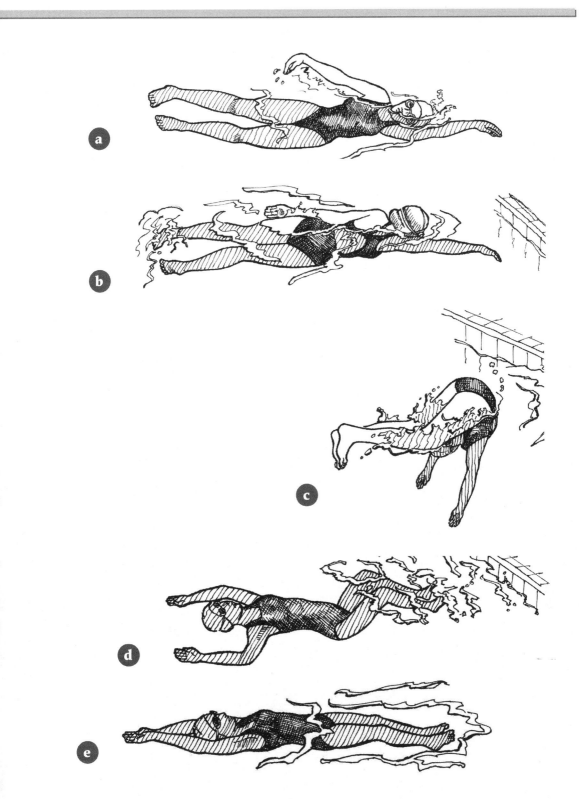

chapter 9

Other Turns and Finishes

Four of the seven turns in competitive swimming require a simultaneous two-hand touch at the wall followed by the turning of the body and pushing off into the next segment of the race. Many swimmers have difficulty making these turns in a smooth manner because of their complexity. Specific skills are required for you to make these turns quickly and efficiently. Mastering certain details and correcting faults can make a significant difference. This chapter addresses the basic mechanics necessary to make these turns effectively, then covers each one specifically.

These drills will focus on

- touching and releasing quickly from the wall,
- developing the proper sequence of steps in making an effective turn,
- Attaining a streamline position off the wall, and
- finishing into the wall or touch pad in a streamline position.

This chapter also addresses the backstroke-to-breaststroke turn, which only requires a one-hand touch. While considerable variation is possible in the execution of this turn, a basic style and the reverse flip are both presented. Once you master this approach, you can then consider more advanced styles.

Purpose

To finish the breaststroke properly.

Procedure

The most common error is for swimmers to take more, shorter strokes as they approach the wall instead of taking fewer strokes and a strong kick and glide into the wall.

1. Start from 10 to 12 yards away from the wall. Swim breaststroke at full speed toward the wall (a). When you reach the flags, try to take fewer strokes to the wall.

2. On the last stroke, get your arms completely stretched out in front of you in a streamline position as you kick and glide into the wall.

3. Drive your head down into the streamline as you finish into the wall. Your fingertips should touch the wall underwater (b). Remember that your hands must touch the wall at the same time. Otherwise, you could be disqualified from a race.

Focus Points

- Finish in a streamline.
- Touch the wall underwater.

Tips

- Practice the breaststroke kick underwater while holding a streamline position with your arms. See how far you can glide for each kick.
- Practice kicking into the wall underwater from about 5 to 10 yards away. Get a feel for how much distance you can cover with each kick.

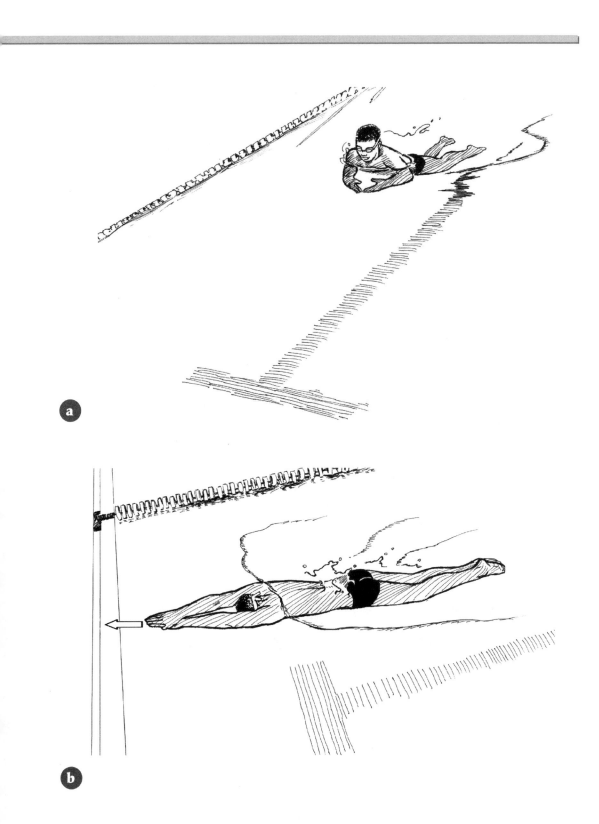

Purpose

To understand the basic mechanics for the two-hand touch turn. This drill applies to four turns: butterfly-to-butterfly, butterfly-to-backstroke, breaststroke-to-breaststroke, and breaststroke-to-freestyle.

Procedure

All of these turns require you to roll a little to the side once you have touched the wall with both hands together. You should never release both hands from the wall at the same time. You should have a two-step release of the hands. The first hand to release goes underwater; the second hand to release travels over the water. Follow these steps:

1. Touch the wall with both hands (a), bring your knees in under your chest (b), and place your feet on the wall.
2. With one arm, pull an imaginary ripcord from the wall and turn to the side. Roll the same shoulder back (c).
3. Push your head underwater.
4. Throw the trail arm past your head so that your hands come together (d).
5. Push off underwater and streamline.

Focus Points

- Practice the steps slowly and in order.
- On the butterfly-to-backstroke turn, drive the arm back directly over your head. On the other turns, throw more to the side and in front of your face, similar to a freestyle recovery.
- Remember the pattern: touch, turn, under, throw, push.

Tip

As you increase speed, try to release the first hand as quickly as possible.

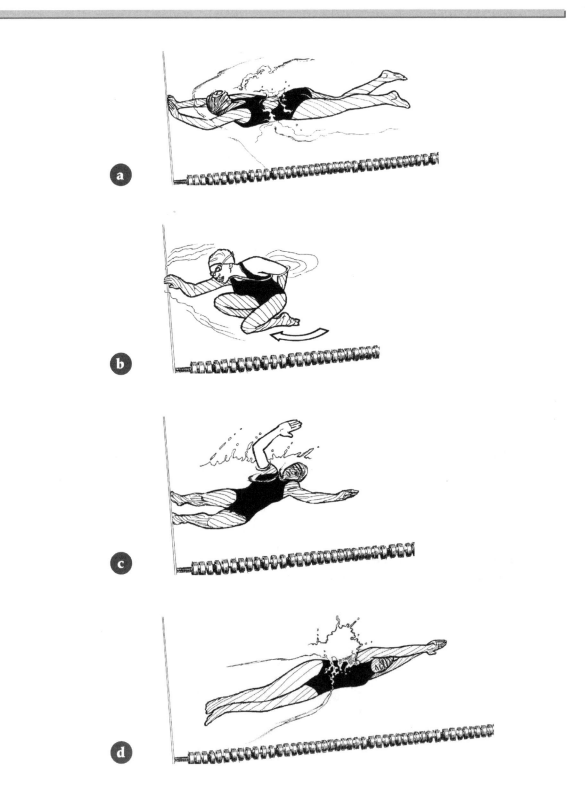

102 BREASTSTROKE-TO-BACKSTROKE DRILL TURN

Purpose
To develop the basic mechanics of the two-hand touch turn.

Procedure
This is a drill turn only, but it will help you develop the basic mechanics. It is the simplest way to practice the turn mechanics.

1. Start from 10 to 12 yards away from the wall. Swim breaststroke at full speed toward the wall. When you reach the flags, try to take fewer strokes to the wall.
2. On the last stroke, get your arms completely stretched out in front of you in a streamline position as you kick and glide into the wall (a).
3. Drive your head down into the streamline as you finish into the wall. Your fingertips should touch the wall underwater.
4. Touch the wall with both hands, bring your knees in under your chest, and place your feet on the wall (b, c).
5. With one arm, pull an imaginary ripcord from the wall, and turn to the side. Roll the same shoulder back (d).
6. Push your head underwater.
7. Throw the trail arm past your head so that your hands come together.
8. Push off underwater on your back, and streamline (e).
9. Kick, and do a backstroke breakout.

Focus Points
- Remember the pattern: touch, turn, under, throw, push.
- Remember, the most important part of any turn is the streamline! Make sure you set yourself up to get an excellent streamline push-off.

Tip
As you increase speed, try to release the first hand as quickly as possible. Then try to pounce off the wall into the streamline.

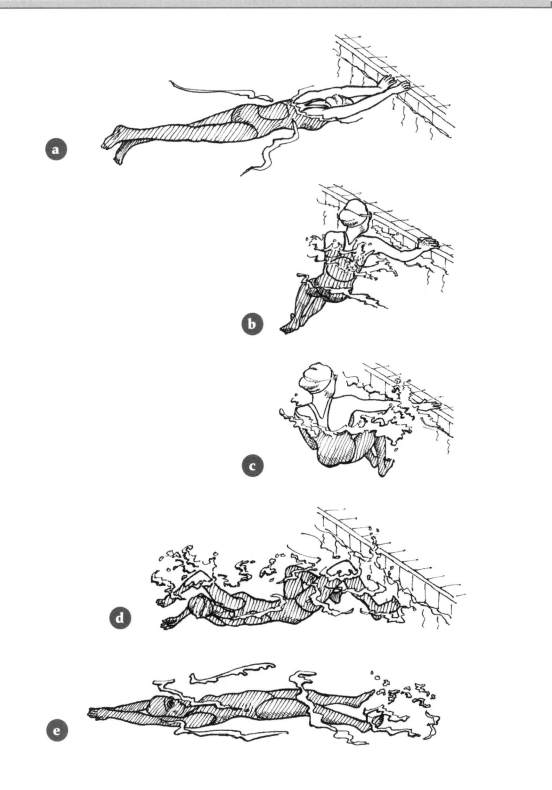

Purpose

To perform a proper breaststroke pullout for the starts and turns. This instruction will give a general guide for good timing in the sequence. A well-executed pullout is a distinct advantage in a race.

Procedure

1. Push off the wall on your stomach, underwater, into a streamline position, facing down toward the bottom (*a*). Hold this position for a count of three.
2. Pull your arms down underneath you, until your hands finish on your legs just above your knees. Pull deeply, with your fingers pointing downward (*b, c*). Hold the finish position for a count of two. You should still be facing down.
3. Bring your hands up to your stomach and bring your heels in to prepare for the breaststroke kick (*d*).
4. Kick your legs, and extend your arms directly forward into a streamline position (*e, f*).
5. Hold the streamline position for a count of one.
6. Begin your breaststroke.

Focus Points

- Remember this pattern of gliding: three, two, one.
- Practice all the steps.
- Maintain consistent depth.

Tips

- This turn has several steps. Practice by adding one step at a time.
- For an advanced variation, see how far you can travel underwater when you perform this drill correctly.

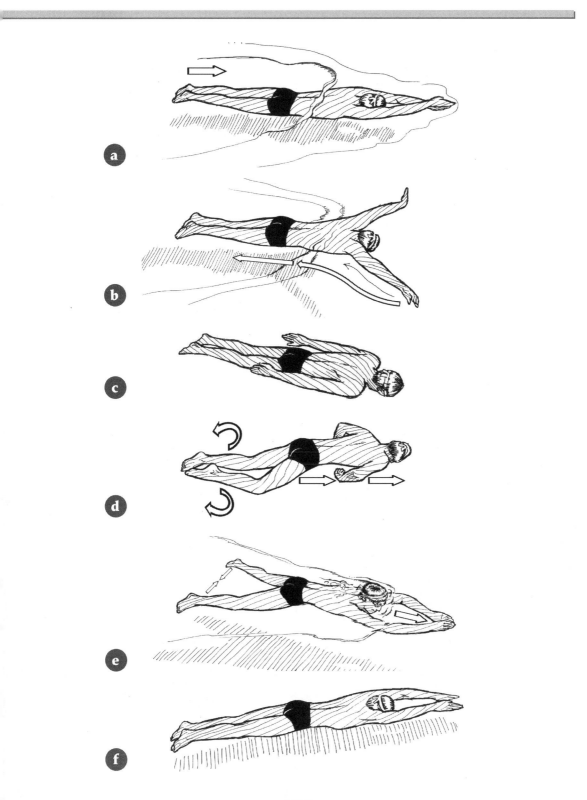

Purpose

To perform a proper breaststroke turn. It is a matter of putting together three parts—the approach, turn, and pullout.

Procedure

1. Swimming the breaststroke, approach the wall.
2. Unlike the finish, let your hands touch next to each other on the wall or on the gutter (a).
3. Perform the two-hand touch turn. Remember the pattern: touch, turn, under, throw, push (b).
4. Hold the streamline position for a count of three, and continue the rest of the pullout (c).

Focus Points

- Keep your head low on the turn.
- Make your shoulders level before you do the pulldown. Otherwise, it is illegal.

Tip

Bring your knees in as fast as you can once you touch to give you a faster turn.

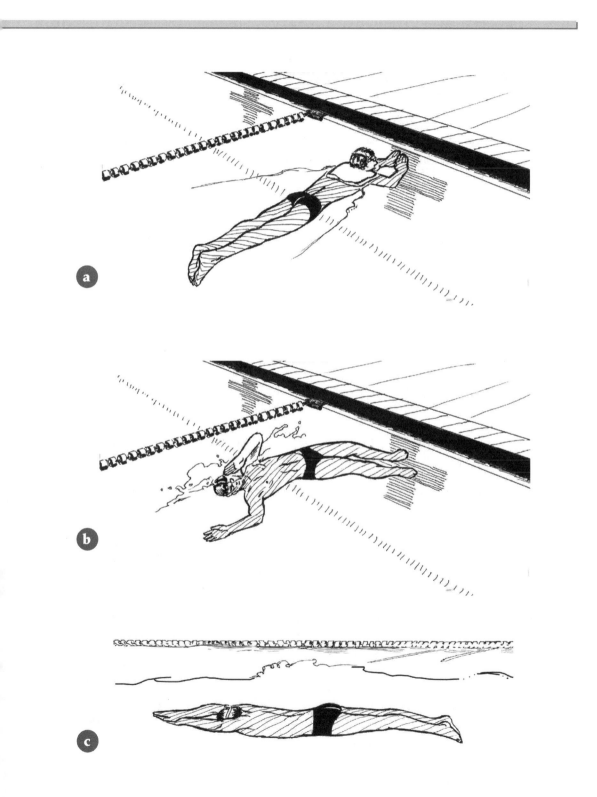

Purpose

To perform a proper finish for the butterfly.

Procedure

Swimmers commonly shorten their strokes as they approach the wall, but it is faster to take fewer strokes and kick in while holding a streamline position rather than take short, choppy strokes to the wall.

1. Start from 10 to 12 yards away from the wall.
2. Swim the butterfly at full speed toward the wall (*a*). Once you get to the flags, try to take fewer strokes to the wall and control your breathing.
3. On your last stroke, get your arms completely stretched out in front of you in a streamline position as you dolphin kick to the wall (*b*).
4. Drive your head down into the streamline as you finish to the wall. Your fingertips should touch the wall underwater. Remember, the hands must touch at the same time. Otherwise, you could be disqualified from a race.

Focus Points

- Finish in a streamline position.
- If you are a little too far to touch right away, kick in.
- Touch underwater.
- Try to take the fewest number of strokes possible for the finish.

Tip

If you have to kick in, accelerate your kick to hyperspeed; make it very quick.

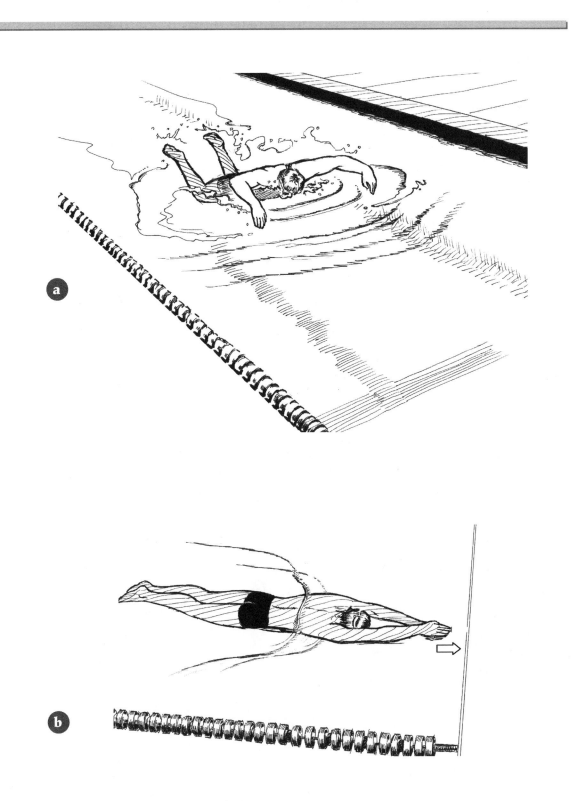

Purpose

To perform a proper butterfly breakout for the starts and turns.

Procedure

Swimmers often fail to streamline and dolphin kick underwater for a sufficient distance.

1. Start from the wall. Push off in a streamline position, and be sure to control your depth *(a)*.
2. As soon as you reach the fully extended streamline, begin to dolphin kick at a very quick pace.
3. Get in at least three kicks before beginning your pulling action to start the stroke.
4. Control your depth so that you break the surface just as you finish pulling on the first stroke *(b)*. Also, control your breathing for the first two or three strokes.

Focus Points

- Keep a tight streamline.
- Maintain quick kicking.
- Travel 5 to 10 yards underwater as quickly as you can.

Tip

Practice dolphin kicking underwater in a streamline as far as you can go. It will help to build up your breath control during the breakout.

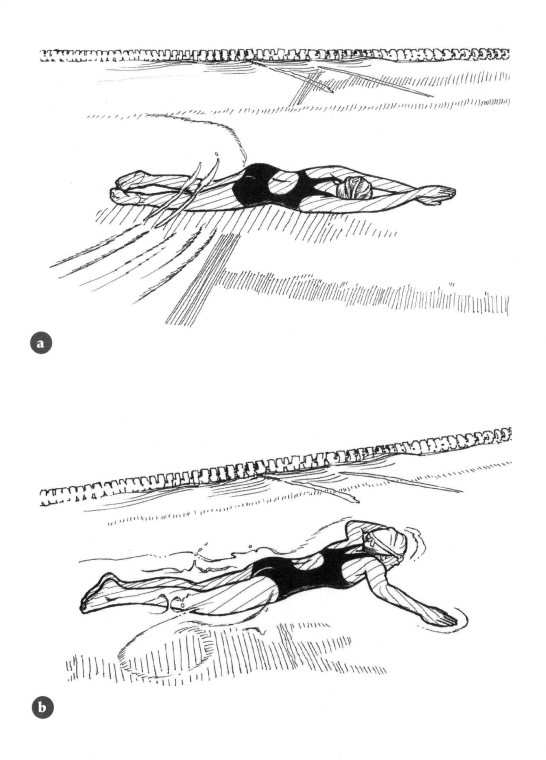

Purpose

To perform a proper butterfly turn. It is a matter of putting together three parts—the approach, turn, and breakout.

Procedure

1. Start 10 to 12 yards away from the wall. Swim the butterfly at full speed toward the wall.
2. Unlike the finish, let your hands touch next to each other on the wall or on the gutter (a).
3. Perform the two-hand touch turn (b). Remember the pattern: touch, turn, under, throw, push.
4. Get into the streamline position, and perform the breakout (c).

Focus Points

- Keep your head low on the turn.
- Be sure that your shoulders are level before you do the pulldown on your first stroke. Otherwise, it is illegal.

Tip

Bring the knees in as fast as you can once you touch the wall to give you a faster turn.

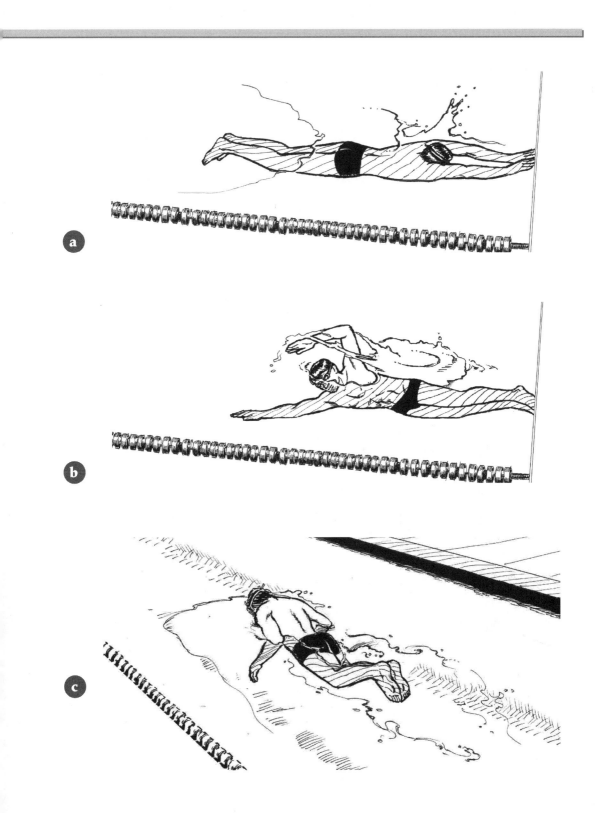

Purpose

To perform a proper butterfly-to-backstroke turn.

Procedure

The most common error in the butterfly-to-backstroke turn is releasing both hands from the wall at the same time. The mechanics for the turn are the same as the other two-hand touch turns.

1. Start 10 to 12 yards away from the wall. Swim the butterfly at full speed toward the wall.
2. Let your hands touch next to each other on the wall or on the gutter (*a*).
3. Perform the two-hand touch turn (*b and c*). Remember the pattern: touch, turn, under, throw, push. (But this time remember to throw directly over-head.) On this turn, the feet will not need to twist on the wall, just the shoulders.
4. Get into the streamline position, and perform the backstroke breakout (*d*).

Focus Points

- Keep your head low on the turn.
- Lean your head straight back after the touch.
- Roll your shoulders so that you push off a little on your side.
- Drive the arm back directly over your head.

Tips

- Bring your knees in as fast as you can once you touch to give you a faster turn.
- Watch your hand release from the wall, and drive over your head.

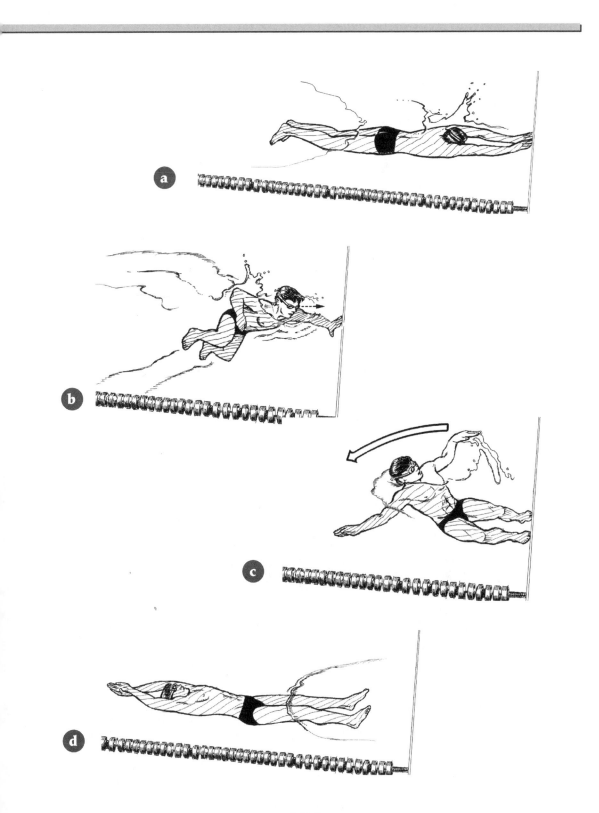

Purpose

To perform a proper backstroke-to-breaststroke turn.

Procedure

The backstroke-to-breaststroke turn has several variations. The open turn, described next, is the simplest, and it is quite effective.

1. Start 10 to 12 yards away from the wall. Swim the backstroke at full speed toward the wall.
2. If there is a gutter, rotate your hand on the final stroke so that your palm is facedown and your thumb extends downward. The fingers will then slide over the gutter wall.
3. Grab the wall with one hand, and pull your feet in underneath you so that you can place your feet on the wall (a).
4. Drop your head underwater, throw your arm, and streamline into your breaststroke pullout (b).
5. If there is no gutter, position your hand on the final stroke so that your fingers are pointing to the opposite side and your thumb is pointing up. Use your hand to push away from the wall as you position your body for the push-off.

Focus Points

- Keep your head low on the turn.
- Use just one arm to perform the turn.

Tips

- Bring your knees in as fast as you can once you touch to give you a faster turn.
- Try not to twist too much on the wall. It is all right to be a little on your side; in fact, it is a lot faster. Just remember that your shoulders have to be level by the time you do your pulldown.

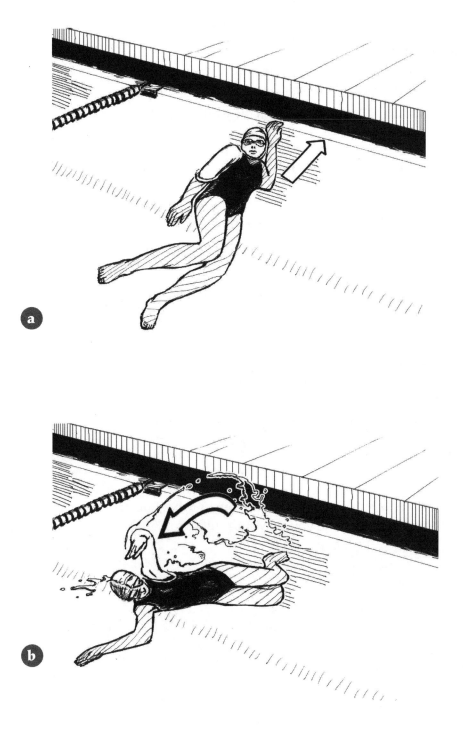

110 BACKSTROKE-TO-BREASTSTROKE REVERSE FLIP TURN

Purpose
To perform the reverse flip turn for backstroke-to-breaststroke.

Procedure
This is an advanced turn. If executed properly, it can be remarkably faster—usually by 0.8 to 1.1 seconds!

1. Start 10 to 12 yards away from the wall. Swim the backstroke at full speed toward the wall (a).
2. On the final stroke, drive the hand down low to place the palm on the wall about a foot or two below the surface. Your fingers will be pointing downward. As you take this last stroke, push your head underwater as well.
3. As soon as your hand reaches the wall, push away from the wall and begin to do a reverse somersault in a tuck position, driving the knees in toward the chest (b). Flip all the way over to place your feet against the wall. Your body will now be prepared to push off into a streamline (c).
4. Push off the wall into a streamline, and perform a breaststroke pullout (d).

Focus Points
- Drive the hand low on the last stroke of the backstroke so that your hand placement is low enough to aid in the flip.
- Get your head underwater on the last stroke.
- Be sure to drive the knees in hard in doing the somersault.

Tips
- Bring your knees in as fast as you can once you touch to give you a faster turn.
- Anticipate the wall once you flip over so that you can punch off the wall quickly.

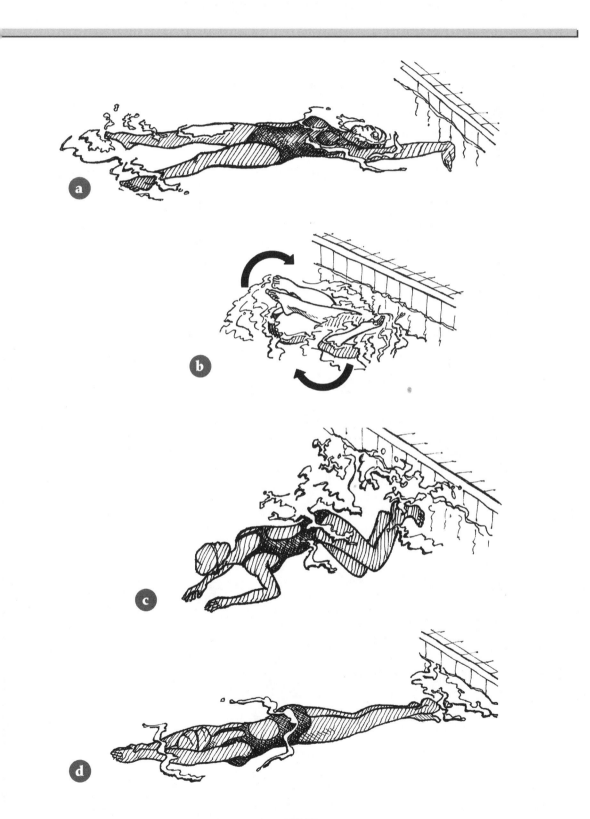

Purpose

To perform a proper breaststroke-to-freestyle turn.

Procedure

1. Start 10 to 12 yards away from the wall. Swim the breaststroke at full speed toward the wall.
2. Let your hands touch next to each other on the wall or on the gutter (*a*).
3. Perform the two-hand touch turn (*b*). Remember the pattern: touch, turn, under, throw, push. Try to push off mostly on your side.
4. Get into the streamline position and do the freestyle breakout (*c, d*). Control your breathing for at least two strokes.

Focus Points

- Keep your head low on the turn.
- Control your breathing for the first two strokes of the freestyle.

Tips

- Bring your knees in as fast as you can once you touch to give you a faster turn.
- The most common error for this turn is no streamline. This turn starts the final leg of the individual medley when most swimmers are tired. A great streamline here is a distinct advantage.

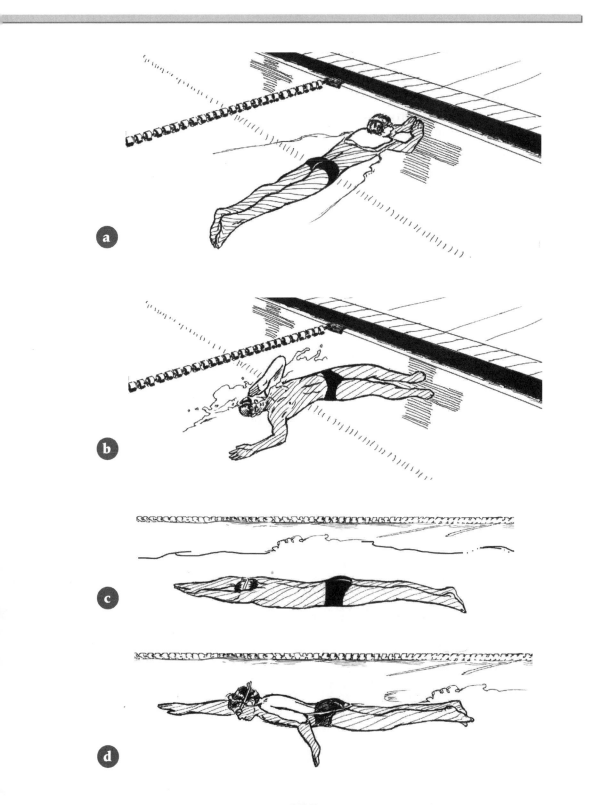

Purpose

To perform a proper freestyle finish.

Procedure

The most common errors by swimmers include breathing inside of the last 5 yards, lifting the head prior to the finish, gliding into the wall, and finishing on top of the wall instead of into the wall or touch pad.

1. Start 10 to 12 yards away from the wall. Swim freestyle at full speed toward the wall.
2. Keep your eyes focused down. Control your breathing from at least the time you pass the flags to the wall.
3. On the last stroke, extend and reach for the wall with one hand touching it underwater. Don't stop kicking. Your fingertips should touch first. Keep your eyes focused down (a, b).

Focus Points

- Control your breathing.
- Kick aggressively.
- Touch underwater.
- Keep your head down.

Tip

If you focus on your competitors during the finish, you lose focus on your own finish. Stay focused on the finish.

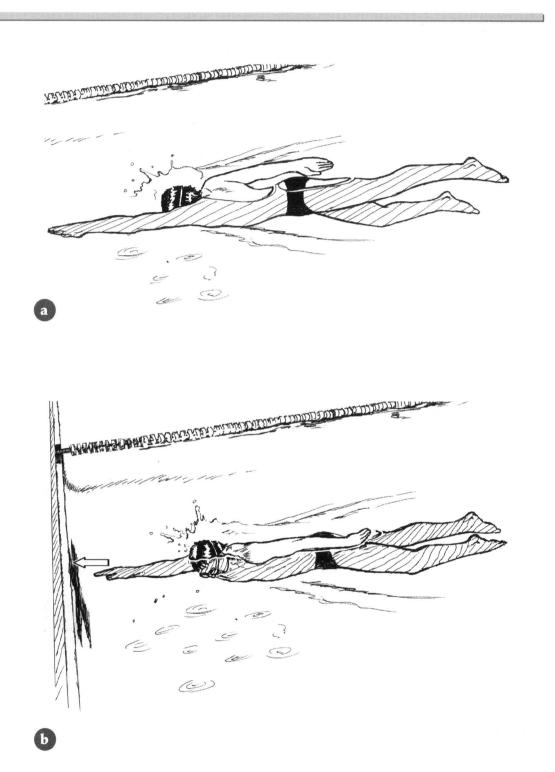

chapter 10

Starts

"Swimmers, take your mark. . . ." Then the gun or horn sounds! Watching a swimmer with a great start is like watching a true act of beauty: quick release, tremendous launch through the air, smooth entry, tight streamline, and rapid travel through a great distance underwater, then coming up well ahead of the pack. If performed well, the start can make a significant difference in the outcome, especially in the sprint races. Conversely, a poor start can leave a swimmer well behind.

These drills concentrate on

- developing leg strength and power,
- discovering your balance point when starting from the blocks, and
- attaining a tight streamline position and controlling the depth of your dive.

The drills in this chapter help you make stronger and faster starts. All of these drills are a lot of fun as well. Swimmers seem to always like practicing starts!

Purpose

To develop explosive leg power for the starts from the blocks.

Procedure

There are two main positions for setting up on the blocks: the traditional start with both feet forward, and the track start with one foot forward and the other foot back a little. Either setup can be effective. It depends on the individual.

1. Place your feet at the edge of the block. For this drill it is usually better to have both feet forward instead of a track start.
2. Bending your knees and using your arms to swing forward, jump from the block into the pool, and land feet first as far into the pool as you can *(a, b)*.
3. Extend your feet as you leave the block so that you spring off your toes.

Focus Points

- Keep your head forward.
- Get as much distance as possible. Use those legs.

Tips

- Practice jumping rope and standing broad jumps to increase your leg strength and jumping ability.
- Have someone measure your distance.

Purpose

To develop the mechanics of quickly extending the body into the streamline position. This drill will prepare you for a clean entry into the water from the blocks.

Procedure

1. Stand on the deck or in the water. Position your feet a few inches apart.
2. Bend the knees, and bring the hands down your legs below your knees. Keep the arms straight (*a*).
3. Begin the movement of the jump by bringing the arms together in front of you and swinging them upward as you jump up into a streamline position (*b*). Jump as high as you can (*c*).
4. Hold the streamline position as you land safely.
5. Repeat at least 10 times.

Focus Points

- Swing the arms forward and upward while keeping the arms straight. The bigger the arm swing, the more momentum you build for the jump.
- Stay balanced, and return to the same spot that you left from.

Tip

Stand in shallow water underneath the flags so that you can jump up and touch them. However, don't look for the flags when you jump; make sure your head stays in the streamline position.

Purpose

To take the next step in developing the start and practice getting into a stream-line position as quick as possible off the blocks.

Procedure

This drill uses the same action as the standing streamline jumps, except you are on the blocks and jump up and out so that you land in the water.

1. Stand on the blocks. Position your feet a few inches apart with the toes over the edge.
2. Bend the knees, and bring the hands down your legs below your knees. Keep the arms straight.
3. Begin the movement of the jump by bringing the arms together in front of you and swinging them upward as you jump up into a streamline position (*a*). Jump forward and as high as you can.
4. Hold the streamline position as you land safely. Try to have a clean entry so that your body is completely straight (*b, c*).
5. Repeat at least 10 times.

Focus Points

- Swing the arms forward and upward while keeping the arms straight. The bigger the arm swing, the more momentum you build for the jump.
- Get completely stretched out into a streamline, and land feet first.
- Keep the head looking forward only.

Tip

Have a coach use a shepherd's crook or pole to attach a target of some sort that you can jump up to and touch safely. However, don't look for the target when you jump; make sure your head stays in the streamline position.

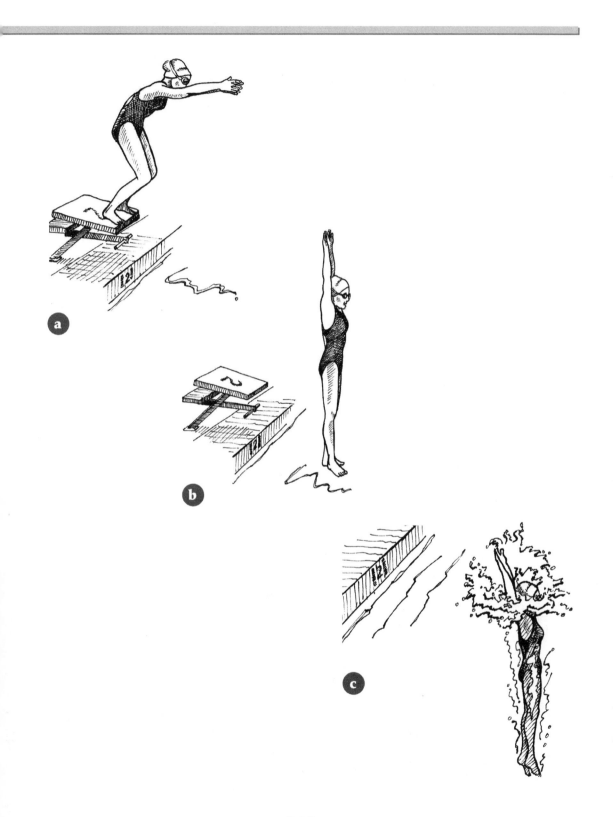

Purpose

To provide a sensory target to aid in the movement of quickly setting up the streamline off the blocks.

Procedure

This drill is advanced and requires the assistance of a coach. You perform the exact same action as the previous drill. However, you knock away the noodle with your arms as you jump.

1. Stand on the blocks. Position your feet a few inches apart with the toes over the edge.
2. Bend the knees, and bring the hands down your legs below your knees. Keep the arms straight (*a*).
3. Your coach will hold a noodle about waist height and about 2 feet in front of you.
4. Begin the movement of the jump by bringing the arms together in front of you and swinging them upward as you jump up into a streamline position (*b, c*). Knock the noodle away as you jump. Jump forward and as high as you can.
5. Hold the streamline position as you land safely. Try to have a clean entry so that your body is completely straight.
6. Repeat at least 10 times.

Focus Points

- Swing the arms forward and upward while keeping the arms straight. The bigger and faster the arm swing, the more momentum you build for the jump. Knock the noodle away with a hard swing.
- Get completely stretched out into a streamline, and land feet first.
- Keep the head looking forward only.

Tip

For the coach: Stand on the side of the deck, and attach the noodle to a pole so that you can position it properly. Oh, be prepared to get wet!

Purpose

This drill is designed to teach the mechanics of the release and body entry. If done properly, it is just like a butterfly entry.

Procedure

1. Position yourself in the water facing away from the wall; your hands are behind you holding the gutter wall, and your feet are up high on the wall *(a)*.

2. Lunge forward and slightly above the surface as you release from the wall. Your arms will travel forward just like a butterfly recovery *(b)*.

3. As your hands come forward and together, get your forehead down and dive into the water, just as you would for the butterfly *(c)*.

4. Immediately reach a tight streamline position. You should have a clean entry.

5. If you time it properly, you can perform a small dolphin kick as your feet enter the water.

Focus Points

- Get your head down quickly as you enter the water.
- Punch a clean hole into the water as you enter.
- Get into a tight streamline right away.

Tip

Try diving over a noodle or some other soft obstacle.

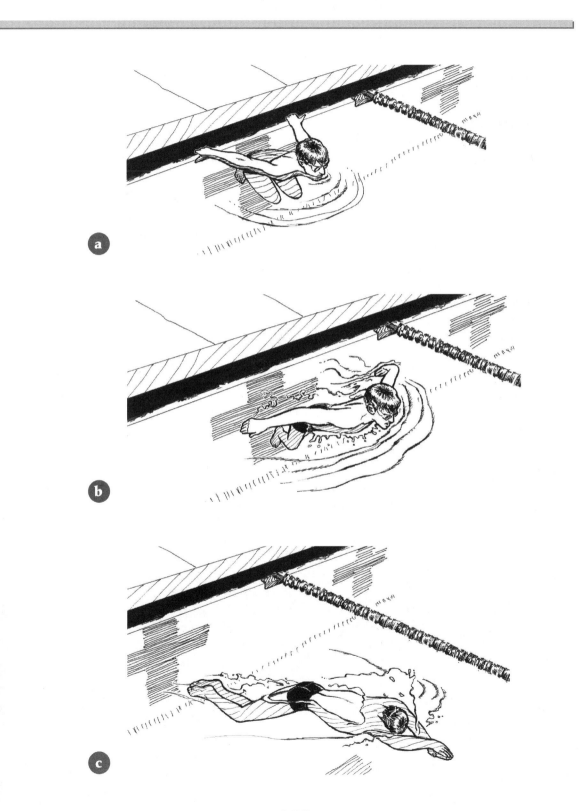

Purpose

To combine the mechanics from the two previous drills in performing a basic dive.

Procedure

1. Stand on the edge of the deck, and come down to take your mark. You may have either both feet forward or use a track start with the feet staggered (a).
2. Roll forward slowly until you can no longer stay on the deck.
3. Release, and dive forward by extending over the water, throwing your arms forward and reaching a tight streamline position as you enter the water (b, c).
4. Try to punch a clean entry into the water.

Focus Points

- Roll forward, then release.
- Reach the streamline as you enter the water.
- Punch a clean entry.

Tip

Practice diving over a noodle, through a hula hoop, or both on the surface of the water.

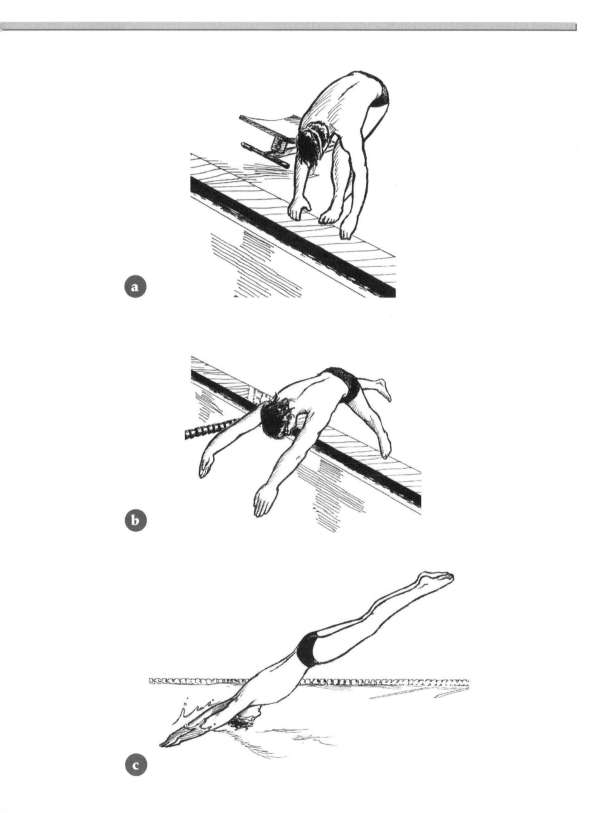

Purpose

To provide a sensory target to aid in the movement of quickly setting up the streamline as you dive.

Procedure

This drill is advanced and requires the assistance of a coach. You perform the exact same action as the previous drill. However, you knock away the noodle with your arms as you dive.

1. Stand on the edge of the deck, and come down to take your mark. You may have either both feet forward or use a track start with the feet staggered (a).
2. Roll forward slowly until you can no longer stay on the deck.
3. Release, and dive forward by extending over the water, throwing your arms forward, knocking the noodle away and reaching a tight streamline position as you enter the water (b, c).
4. Try to punch a clean entry into the water.

Focus Points

- Roll forward, then release.
- Knock the noodle away as hard as you can.
- Reach the streamline as you enter the water.
- Punch a clean entry.

Tip

For the coach: Stand on the side of the deck, and attach the noodle to a pole so that you can position it properly. Again, be prepared to get wet!

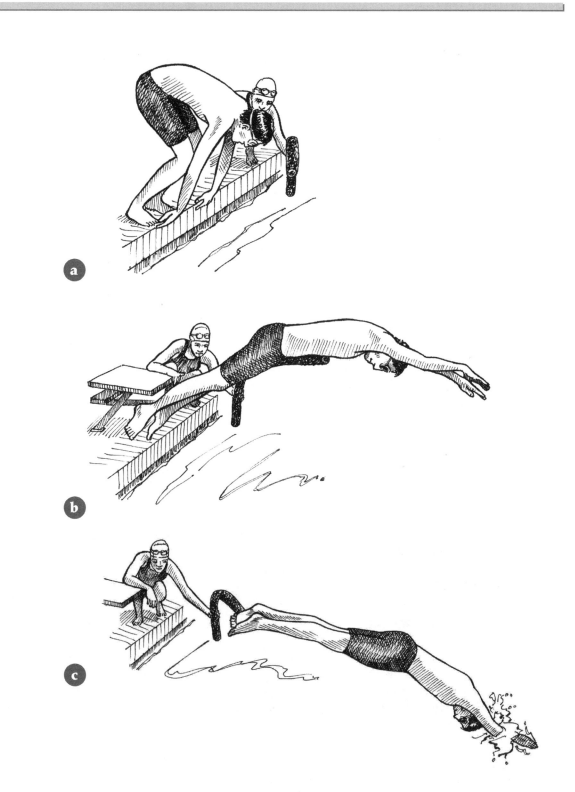

Purpose

To establish getting into good body position on the blocks in preparation for the dive.

Procedure

You can do this drill with either the traditional setup or track start setup (see explanation of track start on page 244). It ultimately depends on individual preference.

Traditional start setup (a):

1. Step forward to the front of the block, and place your feet wide with your big toes curled over the edge.
2. With the knees slightly bent, reach down with your hands until your fingertips are just under the front bottom edge of the block. Barely grab the edge of the block so that it's like a finger hold in rock climbing.
3. Be sure to balance your body so that you are almost falling forward. Your hips should be up and forward.

Track start (b):

1. Stand with your heels at the back edge of the block.
2. Step forward with one foot only, and place that foot with your big toe curled over the edge.
3. With the forward knee slightly bent, reach down with your hands until your fingertips are just under the front bottom edge of the block. Barely grab the edge of the block so that it's like a finger hold in rock climbing.
4. Push the heel of the back leg up, and keep the knee of the back leg only slightly bent.
5. Be sure to balance your body so that you are almost falling forward. Your hips should be up and forward.

Focus Points

- Barely grab the block to allow you to release quickly.
- Balance forward to set up the quickest release and launch from the block.

Tip

Practice getting into position smoothly and consistently. Have a coach give the command, "Take your mark," and get your body into a stable position right away.

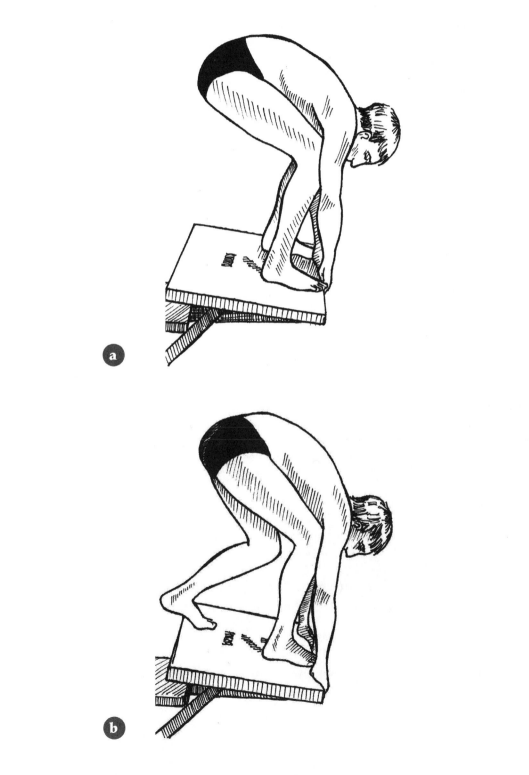

Purpose

To combine the setup with the launch, getting into a streamline position before entry into the water.

Procedure

In this drill you set up first and then launch from the blocks.

1. Stand on the edge of the blocks, and come down to take your mark (*a*).
2. Stay in position until the command to go (or horn) is given.
3. Release, and dive forward by extending over the water (*b*).
4. Recover your arms forward, and reach a tight streamline position as you enter the water (*c*). Try to punch a clean entry into the water.

Focus Points

- Reach forward with your arms to get into a tight streamline as quickly as possible.
- Reach the streamline as you enter the water.
- Punch a clean entry.

Tip

Practice diving over a noodle or other soft obstacle or through a hula hoop on the surface.

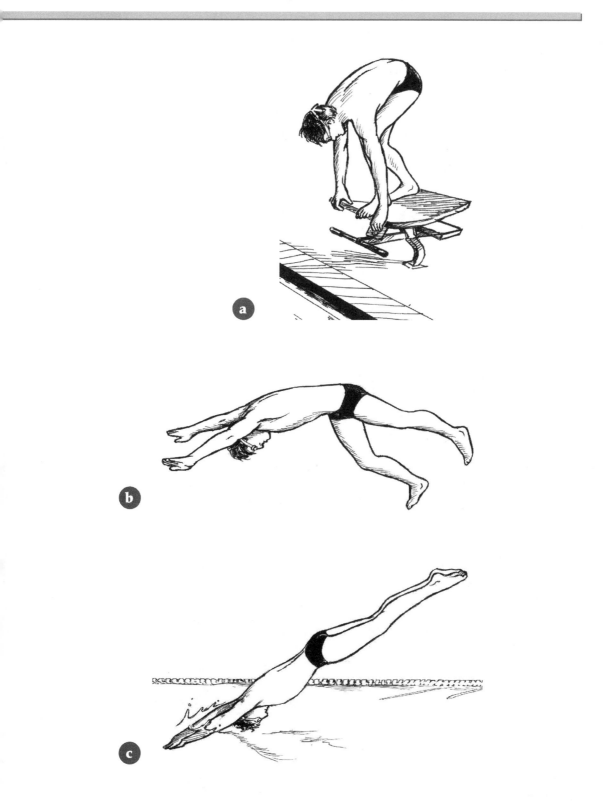

Purpose

To provide a sensory target to aid in the movement of quickly setting up the streamline as you dive.

Procedure

This drill is advanced and requires the assistance of a coach. You will be doing the exact same action as the previous drill. However, you will be knocking away the noodle with your arms as you dive.

1. Stand on the edge of the blocks, and come down to take your mark (a). You may have either both feet forward or use a track start with the feet staggered.
2. Stay in position until the command to go (or horn) is given.
3. Release, and dive forward by extending over the water (b).
4. Throw your arms forward, knocking the noodle away and reaching a tight streamline position as you enter the water (c). Try to punch a clean entry into the water.

Focus Points

- Be completely stable when you take your mark.
- Knock the noodle away as hard as you can.
- Reach the streamline as you enter the water.
- Punch a clean entry.

Tip

For the coach: Stand on the side of the deck, and attach the noodle to a pole so that you can position it properly. Again, be prepared to get wet!

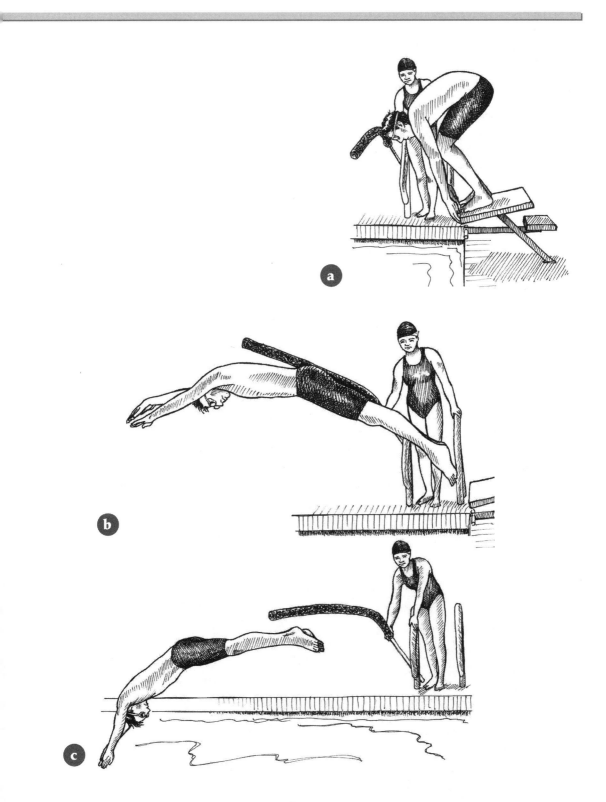

Purpose

To develop the proper path in the air and in the water to gain the greatest speed for the racing starts.

Procedure

The start is the fastest part of the race. The fastest part of the start is when you travel through the air. The second fastest part of the start is the streamline upon entry into the water.

1. Set up on the blocks (a).
2. Take your mark
3. Launch on command (b).
4. Enter the water in a streamline, and hold the streamline position without kicking or pulling (c). However, if you time it properly, you can have one dolphin kick as you enter the water. Continue traveling through the water as far as you can go until you break the surface, then stop (d).
5. Measure how many sections of the lane rope past the flags that you were able to travel. The greater the number, the better your streamline entry.

Focus Points

- Get a great launch.
- Be in a streamline by the time you enter the water.
- Hold the streamline, and slice through the water.

Tips

- Have a contest to see who can travel the farthest in a streamline off the start!
- For the coach: Stand on the side of the pool, and send off your swimmers. Time them for 7 (younger) to 10 (older) yards. Every tenth of a second matters!

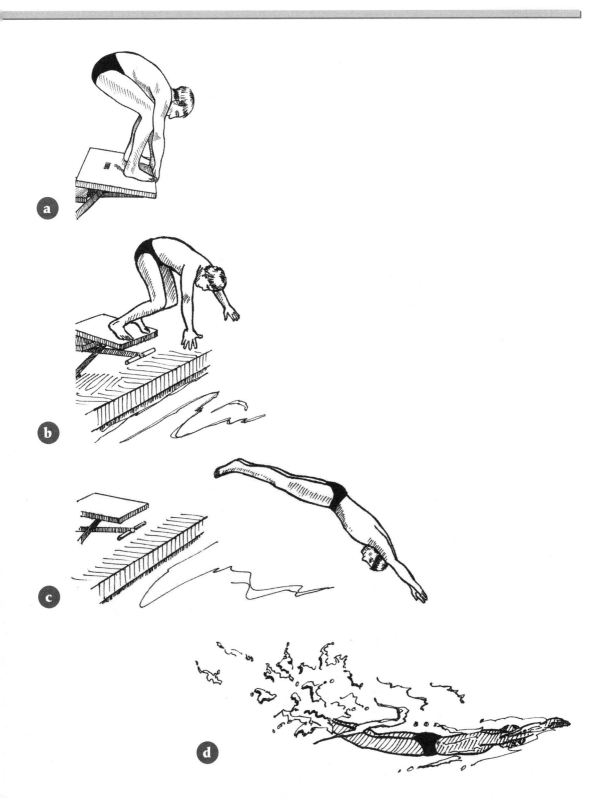

Purpose

To add the butterfly breakout to the dive and entry.

Procedure

This one will be a medium-depth entry.

1. Come down, and take your mark. This time, hold steady at the balance point.
2. On the command "Go," release and enter the water (*a*).
3. Once you enter the water, begin your butterfly breakout with the dolphin kick (*b*).
4. Come to the surface, and swim two or three strokes without breathing (*c*).

Focus Points

- Aim for a tight streamline on entry.
- Control your breathing for the first two or three strokes.

Tip

Do a dolphin kick as you enter the water.

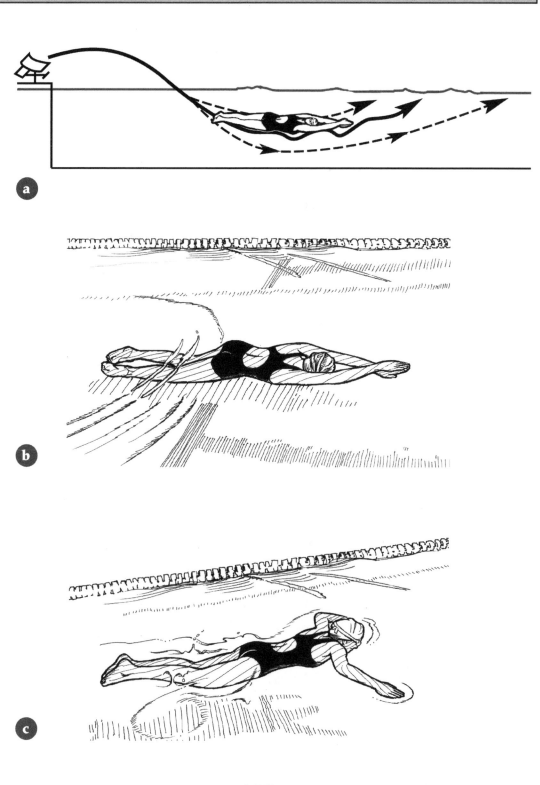

Purpose

To add the breaststroke pullout to the dive and entry.

Procedure

This one will be the deepest of the dives. Generally, most swimmers should reach a depth of about 3 feet.

1. Come down, and take your mark. Hold steady at the balance point.
2. On the command "Go," release and enter the water (a).
3. Once you enter the water, begin your breaststroke pullout by holding the streamline for a count of three.
4. Pull down, and hold for a count of two (b).
5. Kick up, and stretch for a count of one before starting the breaststroke (c).

Focus Points

- Aim for a tight streamline on entry.
- Control the gliding for the pullout. Be patient.

Tip

See how far you can go underwater until you break the surface. Then, have someone time how fast you can get to the same point on repeated efforts.

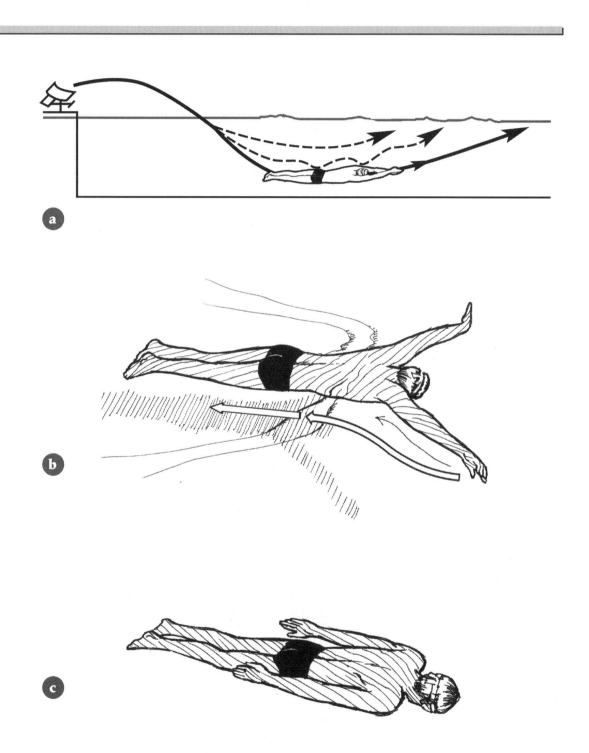

Purpose

To add the freestyle breakout to the dive and entry.

Procedure

This one will be the shallowest of the dives. You should reach the surface fairly quickly once you are in the water, especially on the shorter sprint races.

1. Come down, and take your mark. Hold steady at the balance point.
2. On the command "Go," release and enter the water.
3. Once you enter the water, begin to kick quickly in a tight streamline position (*a*). Bring your head up fairly quickly.
4. Begin the freestyle by pulling down with one arm and breaking the surface (*b*).
5. Control your breathing for at least the first four strokes (*c*).

Focus Points

- Aim for a tight streamline entry.
- Kick very quickly.
- Come up to the surface quickly.
- Control your breathing.

Tip

Do a dolphin kick as you enter the water.

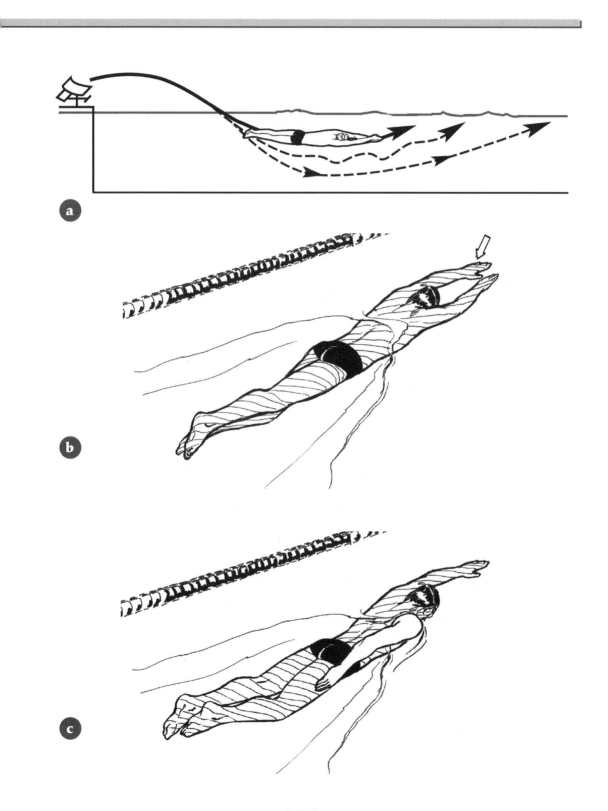

127 BACKSTROKE START SETUP, LAUNCH, AND ENTRY

Purpose
To develop the mechanics for an effective backstroke start.

Procedure
Focus on getting your hips up high above the water as you leave the wall.

1. To learn to arch your back properly, practice in shallow water (4 or 5 feet). From the wall, push off, and immediately perform a back dive into a handstand position. Try to hit the handstand just a few feet away from the wall.

2. Next, have someone hold a noodle at the surface about 3 to 5 feet from the wall (depending on your size). Try to dive backward over the noodle without letting your hips touch it. Immediately reach a streamline position, and kick.

3. To set up for the backstroke start, hold on to the gutter. Place your feet on the wall about shoulder-width apart, approximately 2 feet deep *(a)*.

4. Keep your hips out, away from the wall; do not tuck them in toward the wall.

5. On the command, "Take your mark," bend your elbows and bring your head in toward your hands, but keep your hips out *(b)*.

6. On "Go," release your hands, throw your head back, and spring off the wall. Push your hips up above the surface, and punch a clean streamline on the entry.

Focus Points
- Set up properly. Keep your hips out, away from the wall.
- Arch your back so that your hips clear the surface.
- Get into a tight streamline right away.

Tip
Practice taking off from the wall with your hands holding the gutter handles before moving up to the handles on the blocks.

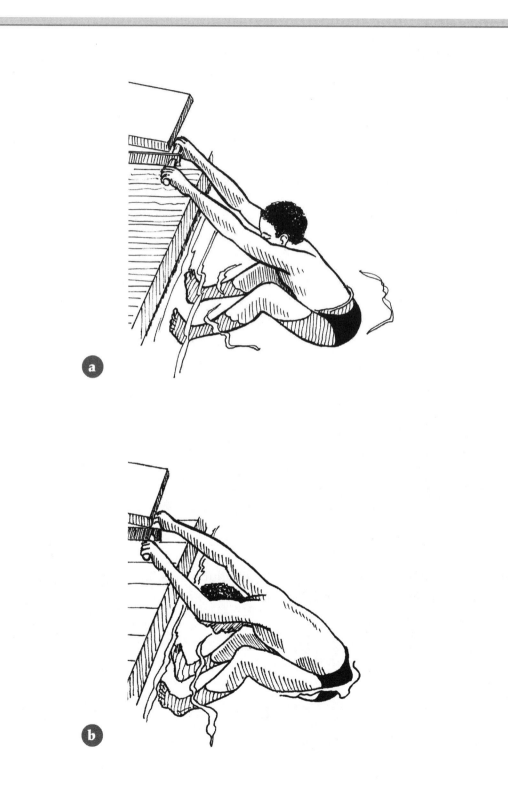

Purpose

To add the backstroke breakout to the launch and entry.

Procedure

The advantage is to have a strong dolphin kick for the underwater work in this start. The rules prohibit traveling more than 15 meters underwater, so you'll need to come up sooner than that distance.

1. Set up on the wall with your hands holding the gutter or the handles of the blocks.
2. On the command, "Take your mark," bend your elbows and bring your head in toward your hands, but keep your hips out.
3. On "Go," release your hands, throw your head back, and spring off the wall. Push your hips up above the surface, and punch a clean streamline on the entry (a).
4. Kick for a count of at least eight (b), then pull one arm down to your side to begin the backstroke arm action (c).
5. Control your depth so that you break the surface just as you finish your first arm pull.
6. Complete about three strokes.

Focus Points

- Perform a clean entry.
- Control your depth.
- Hold a tight streamline for a count of eight or more while kicking.
- Pull only one arm down first before starting your backstroke.

Tip

Once you master this drill with the flutter kick, you can add dolphin kicking in the streamline position and try to get a lot more distance and speed (depending on the individual). However, be sure to control your depth. Remember, you cannot travel more than 15 meters underwater.

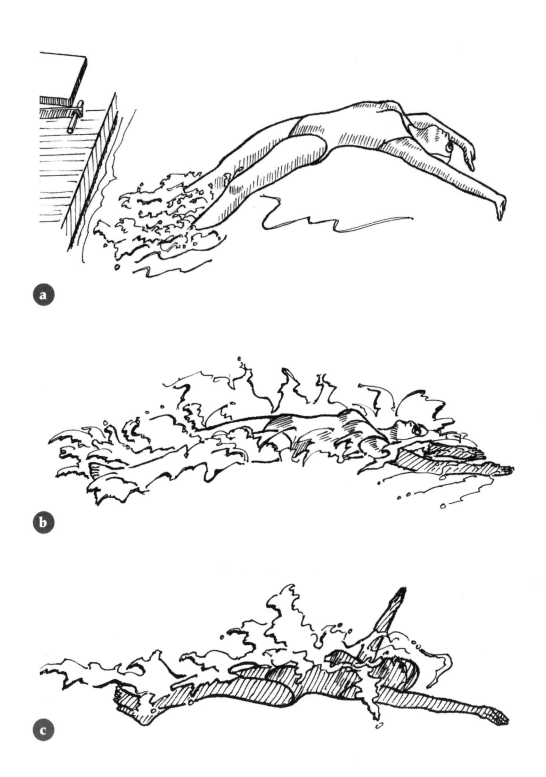

About the Author

Ruben Guzman, a United States Swimming (USS) coach for age-group swimmers, has coached swimming for more than 25 years at the summer recreational, high school, collegiate, and competitive year-round (USS) levels. Some of Guzman's swimmers have advanced all the way to nationals and the Olympic trials. Having served as the "stroke specialist" for the California Capital Aquatics team, Guzman has worked closely with head coach Mike Hastings, an assistant coach on the 1992 United States Olympic Team.

An expert on the mechanisms of the human body, Guzman has trained in physics, kinesiology, anatomy, education, and behavioral changes. He has a master's degree in Public Health and is also a health promotion specialist, consultant, and speaker. Guzman currently serves as the head coach at Christian Brothers High School in Sacramento, California, where he also lives. When he's not coaching or swimming, he enjoys playing basketball and tennis and snow skiing.

More swimming books from the experts

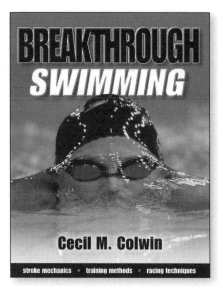

Never before has one book taken such a comprehensive look at the evolution, science, and coaching application of competitive swimming. In *Breakthrough Swimming,* legendary swimming coach and researcher Cecil Colwin provides a rich perspective on the development of the sport and teaches the optimal techniques for all four strokes as well as starts and turns.

262 Pages • ISBN 978-0-7360-3777-8

In *Swimming Fastest,* renowned swim coach Ernest Maglischo reveals the science behind the training methods that led his teams to 13 NCAA Division II national championships and 19 conference championships. This book covers every aspect of competitive swimming, addressing not only the how but also the why of training, accompanied by more than 500 photos and illustrations demonstrating world-class technique.

800 Pages • ISBN 978-0-7360-3180-6

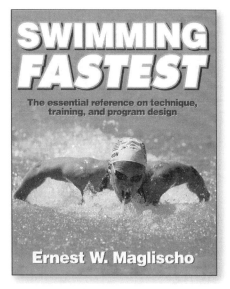

To place your order, U.S. customers call

TOLL FREE 1-800-747-4457
In Canada call 1-800-465-7301
In Australia call (08) 8372 0999
In New Zealand call 0064 9 448 1207
In Europe call +44 (0) 113 255 5665
or visit **www.HumanKinetics.com**

HUMAN KINETICS
The Premier Publisher for Sports & Fitness
P.O. Box 5076, Champaign, IL 61825-5076